MONEY GIRL'S

SMART MOVES TO GROW RICH

Money Girl's

Smart Moves
to Grow Rich

LAURA D. ADAMS

ST. MARTIN'S GRIFFIN NEW YORK

www.stmartins.com

Book design by Kelly S. Too

Library of Congress Cataloging-in-Publication Data

Adams, Laura D.
  Money girl's smart moves to grow rich / Laura D. Adams.—1st ed.
    p. cm.
  ISBN 978-0-312-66262-2
  1. Finance, Personal.   I. Title.
  HG179.A323 2011
  332.024'01—dc22   2010035797

First Edition: January 2011

10 9 8 7 6 5 4 3 2 1

For Adam and Dixie

Contents

CONCLUSION: 20 TIPS FOR PUTTING IT ALL TOGETHER 230

Introduction

I've always enjoyed managing money. As a young high school kid, I couldn't wait to get my own checking account. But as I got older, graduated from college, and went out on my own, I discovered that I had a lot to learn about money. Even working in accounting didn't teach me what I needed to know to stay out of trouble. I fell into the trap that so many people do—living above my means. I rented apartments that I couldn't afford. I spent too much on vacations. I became a shopaholic. My first coworkers in Atlanta, Georgia, made comments about how I always showed up in new clothes and never wore the same outfit twice. They assumed I was living at home with financial support from my parents. I could see the shock on their faces when I told them that, no, I lived on my own. The reality is that I was being supported—not by my parents, but by my credit card!

Later on, I brought my credit card debt into my marriage. As we unpacked big cardboard boxes and started to fill our only bedroom closet, my husband asked, "So, exactly how many pairs of shoes do you have?" It was obvious that my shopping habit would put a squeeze not just on closet space but on our finances as well. After getting extremely anxious about our growing credit card balance, we made a commitment to cut way back and slowly pay off the card. I'll never forget the feeling of accomplishment we had after making the final payment.

Since then I've done a 180—my passion for spending has turned into a passion for saving, investing, and every aspect of personal finance. What I've learned along the way is that you can't manage your money wisely if you don't know how. Many people I talk to about money say something like, "Isn't it a shame that we didn't learn financial stuff in high school?" It *is* a shame, because you don't know what you don't know. Over the years, I went searching for financial answers from lots of books, financial gurus, professional advisers, and eventually graduate school. I accrued so much knowledge that I then began sharing my financial knowledge as the host of the *Money Girl* blog and audio podcast on the Quick and Dirty Tips Network (QDT). As Money Girl, I get all kinds of questions from people who want to take control of their finances but just don't know how. They want to know how to pay off their credit card bills faster, how to choose the best checking and savings accounts, and how to make sure they're saving enough for retirement. My mission as Money Girl is to tell you what you really need to know to master your money, make the right moves, and set yourself up for lasting financial security.

The bottom line is that you're responsible for your own financial well-being, but we live in a world full of complex financial concepts and products. I understand how hard that can be when you're trying to figure out how much to save for retirement, what type of mortgage to get, or how to make investments that aren't too risky. Not only are you managing money in challenging economic times, but there are new tax laws, modernized banking methods, different credit guidelines, and predatory scams to stay on top of. That inspires me to make personal finances easier for you by creating simple explanations, down-to-earth examples, and quick tips that you can put to use right away.

Maybe you're just getting started in the working world and want to make sure you're keeping your money in the right place. Chapter 7 will give you tips on how to grow your money using retirement accounts like IRAs and 401(k)s. Perhaps you're frustrated about your debt, indecisive about your investment choices, unsure about refinancing, or want a faster way to manage your money. If so, keep reading because those are just a smattering of the topics covered in this book. There's a chapter devoted to figuring out where your finances are right now, where you want to take them, and exactly how to bridge the gap. You'll see how easy it is to reorganize your banking so you can earn more money and keep tabs on all your spending with the most modern tools and technology. Chapter 5 will give you hope because there are real ways to reduce and eliminate your debt—I cover them all in detail. You'll get completely up-to-speed on the fundamentals of investing, and by the end of the book you'll know exactly how to save money on your everyday expenses, pick investments, cut your tax bill, buy real estate, pay for education, and lots more. No matter if you're struggling to meet your basic needs or have plenty of income, you'll benefit from this information. If you haven't saved a dime for retirement or are in too much debt (like I was years ago), this book will help you take control of your finances. What you'll find is that once you have good financial knowledge, it's simple to put it into practice and improve your situation.

The purpose of this book is to help you create a richer life. Financial struggles can weigh you down psychologically and hold you back from being who you really want to be. I hope to give you the tips, tools, and inspiration to master your finances, leverage your resources, and reach your highest potential. Small changes in lifestyle and financial routines can create big bank accounts that'll be there when you want to retire, start a business, send a child to college, or give to others in need. Making the right moves now will not only help you manage your money better, you'll grow richer as well.

MONEY GIRL'S

SMART MOVES TO GROW RICH

1

What's Your Money Mind-set?

> If you want to create wealth, it is imperative that you believe that
> you are at the steering wheel of life, especially your financial life.
> —T. HARV EKER, author of *Secrets of the Millionaire Mind*

As Money Girl, I love answering people's questions and sharing helpful financial information and timely tips. In addition to enjoying the nuts and bolts of things like retirement accounts, mortgages, and taxes, I'm also fascinated by the way people think about money. I call it our money mind-set. Your money mind-set—or thoughts about money—is important because it's the precursor to your behavior. In other words, your thoughts turn into actions. If your money mind-set is unhealthy, it only makes sense that you'll probably make some (or a lot of) financial mistakes.

Many people make the same slipups with money over and over again because they're stuck in bad patterns of behavior. They may know an awful lot about making good investments, for example, but can't ever manage to spend less than they make each month and so waste all of their investment knowledge when they have nothing to invest with. The problem isn't a lack of knowledge or the economy—it's them! It's not all gloom and doom, however, because bad financial habits can be fixed. Raising your awareness about them is half the battle. Then you can put the information, tips, and tools in this book into action to take control of your money and make the smart moves needed to get your personal finances back on track and start growing your wealth. In this chapter, I'll help you think about some of the issues that may be getting in the way of your ability to make the most of your money. Let's start by looking at how you've grown to relate to money over the years and bring to light any bad habits you've picked up along the way.

WHAT'S YOUR RELATIONSHIP WITH MONEY?

We usually inherit our money mind-set from our parents or close role models. How we relate to money on a psychological level begins to take shape early in life. That's because young minds can't help but absorb a great deal of their parents' viewpoints. This became obvious to me when I backpacked through Europe with a good friend during the summer after my junior year in college. Neither one of us had a lot of money for the trip, but we decided that we'd travel until our money ran out. Back then, it was realistic for budget travelers to tour Europe on $30 a day. According to my plan, after purchasing flights and train passes, spending no more than $30 a day would keep us afloat in Europe for about a month. My goal was to spend as little as possible so we could stay as long as possible. I was willing to sleep in bunk rooms at youth hostels and to live on bread and water to stretch our funds. But my friend wanted to have more fun, eat fancier meals, and stay at better hotels—even if it meant coming home a little earlier. She simply wasn't as frugal as I was and we both had to compromise. We had the time of our lives—though a shorter time than I would have liked!

I realized that being a little frugal comes naturally to me because that's how I was raised. Even though my parents never actually said, "Laura, you should be frugal with your money," I learned from them by observing their actions. We really didn't talk about money much, but they always focused their resources on what was important to them and never seemed to spend money on whims or fads. That gave me an idea of how to be responsible with money.

Think back to your childhood. If you grew up in a home where there wasn't enough money for the necessities, you might have heard, "We don't have money for that!" or "Do you think money grows on trees?" when begging for that new Barbie or Transformer. If money was tight in your household, you might have grown up thinking that it was hard to earn or that it was impossible to have enough. If your parents constantly fought about how to pay the bills, you might have grown up subconsciously feeling that money was a source of tension or a destructive force in relationships. Or, if you were raised in an affluent family where it was important to keep up the image of wealth, you might still think that you should buy expensive brands, fancy cars, and lead a materialistic lifestyle. Regardless of what kind of household you grew up in, it's likely that your biases and beliefs about money from childhood have stuck with you. Some beliefs—like the importance of delayed gratification—serve us well, but unfortunately, many don't, like the importance of buying expensive brands.

In addition to subconsciously forming some of our strongly held ideas about money when we were only children, the majority of us were taught little or nothing about personal finances during our secondary education. I graduated from a school known for giving a great education. Even though it was, and still is, a fantastic institution, there wasn't a class about money back then. I had a lot of fun making scarves in knitting class (yes, knitting!), but I can't help feeling like my time would have been better spent learning how to balance a checkbook! So don't feel bad if there's a gap in your education when it comes to money matters. Many fellow MBAs I know graduated without being required to take a personal finance class, and they probably have no idea about a lot of everyday money matters. If you lack an educational foundation (formal or informal) for managing your finances, it's very possible that you can lose a great deal of money, no matter how much you have. Conversely, if you make a modest income, but become skilled at money management, you can make the right moves necessary to become quite wealthy over time.

This book will help you form a better relationship with your money, no matter how much of it you have and no matter what your money mind-set is right now. After you read it, I urge you to share your financial knowledge with family members or friends who might benefit from your good sense. Without basic financial education, anyone can create money troubles that are difficult to resolve. When that happens, we run the risk of living in perpetual fear about the state of our finances. That burden can hold us back from living the kind of life we truly want for ourselves and for our families.

BIG, BAD FINANCIAL HABITS (AND LITTLE ONES, TOO)

What stops many people from achieving the bank account and financial stability they dream of are bad spending habits. It's the small things we do day after day, week after week, and year after year that affect our overall financial health. That's good news! That means making little changes is how you'll be able to take total control of your finances. The tips and advice I'll give you in this book won't require that you go out and make all kinds of major changes all at once—that's not realistic. It's the little changes—the baby steps—that will add up to big results with the power to be life changing. But before we can even talk about making small changes, let's figure out if you have any bad financial habits that need to be broken.

The most common bad financial habit is living above your means—that's when your spending is higher than your income. Anyone can spend excessively by taking out loans or making purchases on credit. If you read the introduction to this book, you know that even included me. Living above your means is akin to inhabiting an imaginary place that I call the Dangerous Debt Zone. Unfortunately, it's easy to get there. And if you stay there too long, you will suffer financial injury. If you currently live there, don't worry. Chapter 5 will equip you with the tools you need to get yourself out in no time. But before we can even begin thinking about getting out of debt, we must first realize what got us there in the first place and why we overspend.

See if you recognize yourself in any of these:

- You fall prey to equating self-image with material things
- You crave the thrill of shopping and buying
- You feel entitled to have what others may have

- You're too generous
- You can't delay gratification
- You lack personal responsibility

Let's take a closer look at each of these reasons for overspending so we can put an end to it for good. That's step one on the journey toward financial well-being.

Why We Overspend

As consumers, many of us get brainwashed by the successful branding efforts of product marketers and advertisers. We hear radio commercials and see television, magazine, and billboard ads almost constantly. Most of us are deeply affected by branding, even if we say we're not. Marketers purposefully create brands to act as psychological shortcuts. A psychological shortcut means that the consumer doesn't spend much time considering a given purchase; they just put it in their shopping cart and head to the checkout aisle. I know I'm guilty of doing this every time I go to the grocery store.

There's an irony about the brands we buy. If you think about it, many times the brands we purchase reflect who we want to be, not who we are. For example, if we aren't wealthy but want to be seen as though we are, we buy brands that portray an image of being wealthy, such as Mercedes, Rolex, or Louis Vuitton. We may become attracted to brands and their associated images that we feel disconnected from in our life. For example, if we feel detached from nature, perhaps we buy brands that are associated with the rustic spirit of the outdoors, like Jeep, Patagonia, or The North Face. Or, if we feel old, we might be partial to brands we link to a youthful, vibrant culture like Abercrombie & Fitch or Juicy Couture. What I'm saying is that brands and tastes can be a reflection of what we need the most, and therefore, we may buy them to boost our self-image and self-esteem.

Don't get me wrong, there's nothing wrong with buying any of the great brands that I've mentioned. My point is that if you find that you have a tendency to buy brands that you can't afford, try to understand what's at the core of your behavior. Is it a longing to be unique, part of a crowd, or seen as trendy, elite, or intelligent? Things will never fill our emotional voids. A poor self-image is a bottomless pit that no amount of spending can fill up or make good. Search for ways to fulfill those emotional needs without spending beyond your means. Overspending is not a good way to feel accepted or part of the crowd.

Another reason we may overspend is for the rush that comes from shopping. I'm guilty of this one, too—I can lose hours searching through online sales at my favorite retail sites. For some, shopping produces such a high that it becomes a distraction from everyday life. Frustrations and stress seem to disappear when we're on the hunt for the next best deal. Being aware of this type of addictive behavior is the first step toward conquering it. If you're addicted to shopping, it's important to understand why you buy what you buy. Be conscious of your emotions when you're shopping so you can recognize when a detrimental buying impulse starts to wash over you so that you can stop it.

We may also live above our means due to an "entitlement mentality." If you feel jealous of others or have a sense of entitlement to have what your neighbors or friends have, that may be a root cause of overspending. The truth is that you just might not be able to afford the same car as your neighbor or the same shoes as your best friend. But no matter your level of income or skills, you can create a life that has a safe and secure financial future—as long as you drop your feelings of entitlement.

Overspending also happens when you want to do more for others than you can afford. Do you have relatives who always seem to want more and more from you? Do you overspend on gifts during the holidays or for other special occasions? Do you give money to anyone who knocks on your door and asks for it? It's wonderful to be a generous person when you truly can afford it. But when you go overboard to try to win the affections of others or because you're not clear about your own financial needs, you're not taking good care of yourself.

What if you don't equate your self-worth with the products you buy, you don't get a thrill from shopping, and you don't have a sense of entitlement when it comes to what you buy, but are still overspending? You might have an inability to balance short-term pleasures with long-term gains. Whether it's resisting the temptation to buy something shiny that we really don't need or pushing away a second helping of cake when we're on a diet, the desire for instant gratification is something we battle with every day. Maybe it will help you to keep the reasons you need to practice delayed gratification close to you. How you spend your money reflects your values. Consider putting your values down on paper so you can place them in strategic spots like on your computer, in front of the credit card in your wallet, or in your car, so you'll be reminded of them before blowing money in a way that's not helpful to you or your family.

The last reason many of us overspend is that we have a lack of personal responsibility. Responsibility or accountability can fly out the window when we simply can't or won't accept reality. We can rationalize situations and poor behavior in an attempt to cover up an ugly truth that we don't want to see. Rationalizations always sound good, but we know deep down that they're not the real explanations for why we may do something that's unproductive. I'll share an example with you about a friend who accepted a new sales job. His offer was a low base salary with a high commission in the construction industry. Even though the industry was starting to decline, he was convinced that his income would double within six months. Before getting his first paycheck he went out and bought an expensive car, boat, and lots of new furniture. He was able to buy all of these things by taking out loans and using a credit card. He felt he'd need those things to entertain and impress customers. When the construction business fell off due to the recession, my friend's job wasn't eliminated, but he couldn't generate the big commissions that he'd expected. He should've seen the writing on the wall, sold his expensive toys, and made spending cuts, but he didn't. He felt like a failure and couldn't accept that his big career break was broken. He went further into debt and waited too long to try to find a better-paying job.

Sometimes it takes a severe financial crisis to occur before our personal responsibility gets reawakened. If you have a habit of overspending, look at the specific expenses that push you overboard. Once you uncover the root causes of your overspending, you're making good progress toward overcoming that bad habit.

ONE LAST MONEY SECRET TO GROWING RICH

Before we get started talking about specific information and techniques to make smart moves and grow rich, I'll share a secret with you that only the wealthy know. You begin to take control of your financial reality when you can take full control of yourself—not a moment before. The inability to manage money is actually the inability to manage yourself. So maybe you have some work to do before it's even possible to get on the road to financial security. That's okay, keep reading. My challenge to you is to complete this book, then come back to it again in the near future. You'll rediscover new truths and financial tactics that perhaps didn't mean anything to you before.

A financial transformation occurs when we adopt an entirely new view of money. That's why I asked you to examine your money mind-set at the beginning of this chapter. Stepping outside of the linear idea that work=money=things is the beginning of a transformation. Viewing money only for what it can bring you in terms of possessions is a root cause of financial distress and unhappiness.

Being rich or wealthy is a relative concept. The absolute amount of money you have isn't nearly as important as how you handle your money each and every day. If you maintain a foolish relationship with your money year after year, I can predict your future, and it's not as blissful as it could be. No matter if you're a millionaire with money freely flowing, or if you're making minimum wage, you have the power and ability to set aside enough money to create financial security. My goal in this book is to empower you to achieve your best financial life. Making the most of what you have, and being grateful for it, is truly the secret of financial well-being and happiness.

The next step in your journey to grow richer is to learn the skills you need to change your behavior, become a great money manager, and live within your means. Let's get started.

2

Creating a Financial Plan

> Map out your future, but do it in pencil.
>
> —JON BON JOVI, musician

Now that we've talked about why we might be overspending and not doing a great job managing our money, let's take the first step toward changing that. Improving your financial health is not something that happens overnight, and before you can begin to make changes you have to figure out the following:

1. what your financial situation is today,
2. what you'd like your current and future financial situation to be, and
3. what needs to be done to fill the gap between the two.

If you don't know how to answer those questions, don't worry! That's what I'm here to help you with. Let's start by getting a grasp on your current financial situation. That can be frightening for many people, because they don't like their situation or don't want to face it. However, embracing reality makes you better able to make positive changes. Let's start off by creating an important tool that you can use throughout your life to help you gauge your level of financial fitness. Then you'll learn how to set important financial goals and get into the nitty-gritty about how to really make them happen.

KNOW YOUR NET WORTH

The tool I'd like you to create is called a Personal Financial Statement, or PFS. Everyone should create and update their PFS on a regular basis, annually or even quarterly. It's the best way to get a complete view of your current financial situation and should be your periodic "reality check"—something like stepping on the scale if you're watching your weight. Each time you update your PFS, the purpose is to recalculate your net worth, which tells you a great deal about your overall financial health.

The definition of net worth is summed up in a very simple formula:

Net Worth = Assets − Liabilities

When you subtract your total liabilities from your total assets, you have calculated your net worth. It's really that simple! If you own $350,000 in assets, but have $325,000 in debts, your net worth is $25,000. Net worth is an important number because it reveals your bona fide financial resources at a given point in time. Tracking your net worth keeps you focused on increasing your assets and shrinking your liabilities.

Since everyone's financial situation is unique, there's not a magic net worth number that you should have. The Federal Reserve (federalreserve.gov) keeps track of the net worth of U.S. families in the Survey of Consumer Finances that's published every three years. The most current survey shows that the net worth of all families steadily increased from 2004 to 2007. In 2007, the median net worth of all families was $120,300 (that's the number in the very middle of the data) and the average was $556,300. However, we know that the recession and the general decline in the housing market caused net worth to fall from the figures reported for 2007. When your net worth increases, pat yourself on

Here's a quick and dirty tip: Use this formula as a very rough guideline for your target net worth: [Your age - 25] × [Gross annual income ÷ 5].

the back and know that you're making the right financial decisions.

Calculate Assets and Liabilities

In order to figure out your net worth you must calculate your assets and liabilities. Assets are what you own that have real value, such as cash accounts, stocks, bonds, real estate, vehicles, personal belongings, and money owed to you. Your liabilities, on the other hand, are the opposite of your assets. Liabilities are your financial obligations to others. They could include a mortgage, a car note, a credit card debt, or the $50 you owe your neighbor for losing a bet. Your net worth reveals what you'd have left over if you liquidated all of your assets and paid off all your debts today. You probably wouldn't really do that unless you decided to join a Buddhist monastery, but it's an important financial exercise nonetheless. If you owe more than you own, your net worth will be a negative number. If that's your situation, don't let it upset you too much. Many people, young and old, are in the position of having a negative net worth. Your net worth has nothing to do with your personal worth as a human being—never forget that. But knowing your net worth will help you understand what you need to accomplish to meet your financial goals and dreams.

In addition to calculating your net worth, a good PFS will also contain everything that loved ones would need in the event of your death. One of the best gifts you can give to those you leave behind are organized personal finances. You may want to give a copy of your PFS to your children, parents, or any other close family members who might need access to detailed information about your financial accounts and insurance policies. I like to keep an updated copy of my PFS in a safe-deposit box at a local bank. It's also a useful document to have when applying for credit or loans. But I encourage you to create it and maintain it primarily for yourself and your family. See the sample PFS that I've included—you can also download this document from the Money Girl Web site at http://moneygirl.quick anddirtytips.com under the Recommended Reading sidebar. You may have more or less information to enter, but your goal should be

Here's a quick and dirty tip: Use a spreadsheet format such as an Excel file or a free Google Doc at docs.google.com to create your PFS.

to create a complete and accurate record of all your assets and liabilities. Once created, it should be an evergreen document that you save and update on a regular basis, at least once a year.

To create your PFS, you can use the sample here as a guide or you can list your assets on a blank page or spreadsheet. To the right of each asset, list its estimated value. Try to get as close as you can to an accurate value; you can always revise your estimated valuations at a later time. For now, catalog your possessions and accounts that have monetary value.

Instead of taking a lot of time to list many smaller assets individually, try lumping them together in categories. Include a ballpark estimate for the value of your furniture, antiques, artwork, and collectibles, for example, under a category called "household possessions." Include computers and televisions under an "electronics" category. The idea is to consider what you own that would have real value if you sold it today. Remember that the market value of most tangible assets is usually lower than their replacement value. For example, if you paid $2,000 for your five-year-old computer, you probably could never sell it today for $2,000. So it's best to be conservative with your asset valuations.

For your larger assets like real estate, vehicles, boats, financial securities, or precious metals, spend some time researching their values so you can be as accurate as possible. Kelley Blue Book, at kbb.com, is the best way to find valuations for vehicles. Utilize sites like ebay.com and craigslist.com to find prices for assets like sporting equipment or high-end tools. Get the value of your stocks or mutual fund shares from your last account statement or from a brokerage Web site such as etrade.com or scottrade.com.

A Web site that can help you with your real estate valuations is Zillow.com. Zillow.com creates estimates from data available in the public records, but it admittedly doesn't take everything into consideration such as local market conditions or special features of a

SAMPLE PERSONAL FINANCIAL STATEMENT

ASSETS

Cash on Hand	$ 200
Cash in Checking Accounts	$ 500
Cash in Savings Accounts	$ 1,000
Cash in Money Market Accounts	$ 15,000
Cash in Certificates of Deposit	
Value of Investments (stocks, bonds, mutual funds, ETFs)	
Value of Workplace Retirement Accounts	$ 10,000
Value of IRA Accounts	$ 2,000
Cash Value of Life Insurance	
Surrender Value of Annuities	
Other Investments	
Value of Precious Metals	
Estimated Market Value of Real Estate	$ 300,000
Estimated Value of Vehicles	$ 10,000
Estimated Value of Collectibles	
Estimated Value of Household Items (furniture, sporting equipment, tools)	$ 1,000
Estimated Value of Electronics	$ 500
Estimated Value of Jewelry & Furs	$ 2,000
Money Owed to You	
Other Assets	
TOTAL ASSETS	**$ 342,200**

LIABILITIES

Balance Owed on Mortgages	$ 275,000
Balance Owed on Auto Loans	$ 3,500
Balance Owed on Student Loans	$ 12,000
Balance Owned on Other Loans	
Balance on Home Equity Line	
Balance on Credit Cards	$ 2,000
Balance on Other Credit Lines	
Outstanding Bills	
TOTAL LIABILITIES	**$ 292,500**

TO CALCULATE YOUR NET WORTH:

TOTAL ASSETS	$ 342,200
LESS TOTAL LIABILITIES	$ 292,500
= NET WORTH	**$ 49,700**

GET ONLINE TO GET ORGANIZED

Online tools, such as itaggit.com, can help you get your personal possessions cataloged, organized, and valued. Itaggit has a valuation tool that helps you establish the current market value of an item. Enter your possessions into itaggit.com from an iPhone application, import data from a spreadsheet, add pictures, or export items directly to online marketplaces such as ebay.com and craigslist.com. Itaggit.com even offers valuation reports for estate planning and tax purposes.

property. If you really want to hone in on the market value of your property, it's best to hire a licensed real estate appraiser to do a thorough analysis. But Zillow.com may be a good starting point for your PFS. If you have some expensive jewelry, that's another asset for which you may want the opinion of a qualified appraiser or gemologist. Once you've got all your assets accounted for, create a "total assets" row, perhaps with a cell formula that adds up each individual asset category.

Follow this same procedure for adding your liabilities to your Personal Financial Statement. There are two different types of debt that most people have: installment loans and revolving lines of credit. Installment loans—like mortgages—have specific conditions that must be met until the borrower pays off the full amount. Installment loans are usually secured by an asset, such as real estate or a vehicle, and have an interest rate (either fixed or variable) and a term that specifies the future payoff date. Installment loans are very different from revolving lines of credit. With credit lines, like credit cards and home equity lines of credit (HELOCs), the financial institution agrees to give you a maximum loan amount. If you choose to use any part of the money, you're charged an annual percentage rate (APR) each month on the balance that you carry forward. The interest you owe each month is the minimum payment that you can make without incurring additional interest and late fees.

Enter your current balances for all loans, lines of credit, credit cards, and any notes that you have in your PFS. Also include the rate of interest charged on each debt as well as the maturity or pay-off date of your installment loans. You may be able to get the information by viewing your accounts online. If not, refer back to your most recent account statement or call the creditor for any missing information. Then create a "total liabilities" row, to see the grand total of all your debts. At the bottom of your PFS create a "net worth" row that shows the result of subtracting your total liabilities from your total assets. If you have a lot of debt, this number will likely be negative. Don't get too upset. The point of calculating your net worth is to use the information to help you create a smart plan to improve your finances. The goal is to slowly raise your net worth each year. In chapter 4, which is about money management systems, I'll give you some recommended tools that can help you calculate and monitor your net worth online.

CREATE A FINANCIAL PLAN

Now that you know your net worth, it's time to create a financial plan. Why is a financial plan important? Think of it this way: If you were building a new home, would you pour a concrete foundation before having finalized your house plan? That would be extremely risky and probably leave you with some major design flaws and regrets. Creating a financial plan is just like having a detailed house plan—it shows what you intend to create with your money. It's part of the process of identifying your goals and determining how you're going to manage your money to achieve them. Financial planning may seem boring, but you just have to hunker down and do it if you want to make the smart moves necessary to live a financially secure life. It's possible to get lucky and end up having enough money to reach goals like buying a home or retiring, by chance. But I wouldn't count on it!

Financial planning doesn't have to take a long time or be complex. You don't have to be a financial whiz or have a high-paying job in order to achieve your financial goals. Simply reflect on the big picture of your life. What financial and nonfinancial dreams do you have? A useful exercise is to imagine your life five years from now. Consider where you're living and how you spend your time. In five years, what would you be proud to say that you had accomplished between now and then? Stretch your imagination out further and do the same for your life in ten or twenty years. Then imagine you're on your deathbed with just a few hours left to live. What accomplishments would make you feel good about yourself even in your final hours? These questions can give you important information about yourself and inspire you to begin planning for what truly matters to you. In this chapter we'll discuss how to identify all your financial goals, big and small, so that you know what you're working toward. Then the rest of the book will help you achieve these goals.

How to Set Your Goals

There are three different types of goals to consider when you're doing financial planning: short-term, medium-term, and long-term.

1. **Short-term goals** are those you want to achieve within a year. They could be saving for a vacation, maxing out a retirement account, or buying a new mountain bike, for example. One of the most important and very first short-term goals that I recommend you achieve is to establish an emergency fund. This goal trumps all others and I'll explain why coming up.

2. **Medium-term goals** are those you want to accomplish in the range of one to five years in the future. For many, a year isn't enough time to save up an adequate emergency fund and so that goal might be one of your medium-term goals. Other examples of medium-term goals that you may have in mind are making a down payment on a home, starting your own business, buying a new car, or saving for your children's education.

3. **Long-term goals** are, of course, those you want to achieve beyond five years into the future. The granddaddy of all long-term goals is saving for retirement. I'll give you the basics on how to do that in this chapter. If your kids are young, saving for their education may play into your long-term plans. There are special types of

tax-advantaged accounts that are sponsored by the government to help boost both our retirement and education savings that we'll cover in future chapters.

GOAL #1: AN EMERGENCY FUND

As I mentioned, having an emergency fund should definitely be one of your first financial goals. You could get into real trouble without one. None of us knows what the future holds when it comes to our income, our economy, or our health. It's vital that we hope for the best, but plan for the worst. If you lose a portion or all of your income, you still have living expenses to pay. Unemployment benefits can help you survive a layoff, but that income is only temporary and isn't likely to cover all your expenses.

So, how much emergency money is really enough? Unfortunately, I can't tell you exactly how much you need. The answer varies depending on your personal situation. I recommend that your initial goal is to save six months' worth of living expenses, whether you're single or married. If that sounds completely unrealistic, don't get discouraged—start smaller, with three months or even one month as your goal. If your living expenses amount to $40,000 a year, for example, you could decide to accumulate $20,000 over a three-year period. If you have a savings account that earns 1.5 percent interest, you'd reach your goal by saving $543 a month or $125 a week. At the end of this chapter I'll give you tips for how to save money faster.

Now this is important: The money in your emergency fund should be in addition to what you may already have saved in other accounts such as an Individual Retirement Arrangement (IRA) or a plan at your work, like a 401(k). It's best not to consider money in your retirement accounts as part of your emergency fund. Ideally, you would never have to dip into your retirement funds, even in an emergency situation. Your reserve fund needs to be very accessible so it's best to keep it in cash in an FDIC-insured bank account such as a high-yield savings or money market deposit account. I'll give you much more information about banking accounts in the next chapter.

You can also keep a portion of your emergency money in a safe place in your home. Call me alarmist, but there are catastrophic situations where you might need cash on hand to survive. If widespread power outage or flooding should cause your bank or Internet access to shut down temporarily, for example, you'd be grateful to have some cash stashed at home. Withdrawing money from ATMs (automatic teller machines) could also be problematic in certain situations. If you live in a rural area, your isolation should prompt you to err on the side of caution when it comes to accessing your emergency money. Once you have your reserve fund in place, the security it will give you is amazing!

When You Might Need Extra Savings

Once you have six months' worth of living expenses saved, consider whether you need more. Replacing lost income can take longer than you think it will, depending on your industry, skills, and experience. Whether you have emergency money or not can make the difference between staying afloat financially or sinking into further trouble. Here are some situations that should prompt you to have more than a six-month emergency fund on hand:

- You're married, but only one spouse works
- You live in an older home that could need emergency maintenance
- You have older household appliances that may need to be replaced
- You drive an older car that could need unexpected repairs
- You have high insurance deductibles for health, homeowners, or auto policies
- Your job, industry, or business experiences a downturn
- You plan to purchase a home
- You plan to have children or to adopt
- You have inadequate homeowner's insurance due to living in an area prone to natural disasters or flooding
- You have family members who may become dependent on you

MAKE HAVING INSURANCE A GOAL

An important aspect of being prepared for an emergency is being adequately insured. Many people get into debt because they don't have enough of the right kinds of insurance (or they don't have any insurance at all). As your personal finances improve and your career progresses, it's likely that you'll have more assets and income to protect from unexpected events. Without adequate insurance, a catastrophic event could wipe out everything you've worked so hard to earn. It's not pleasant to think about what bad things could happen, and maybe that's why so many people are underinsured. Part of taking control of your finances is being prepared to deal with situations that may put a drain on your finances. These following seven types of insurance will help you protect yourself and those you love from something unexpected jeopardizing your financial security and happiness:

1. Health insurance is a critical insurance to have. Without it you risk being stuck with a large bill if you have any kind of medical issue from the flu to a broken bone. Even a quick emergency room visit or a basic hospital bill can cost thousands of dollars. Starting in 2014, health care reform will penalize uninsured adults who don't have a valid exemption, such as low income. If you don't have the option to purchase health insurance at work, or if you're self-employed, shop rates at ehealthinsurance.com. Also, don't assume that a workplace option is the best one for you. Review it in light of your family's situation. In some cases it could be better to take a group policy for yourself but to insure your dependents separately, for example. You can shop for health insurance just like any other type of insurance. Compare policies by reviewing all the features and terms carefully. You may opt for a high-deductible health plan that has lower premiums and offers the unique ability to save money for future qualified medical expenses in a tax-advantaged health savings account or HSA. Visit the U.S. Department of Treasury Web site at treas.gov for more information about HSAs.

2. Disability insurance provides replacement income if you're unable to work due to a disability, illness, or accident. Remember that health insurance only addresses your medical bills; it doesn't pay your living expenses, like housing or food, if you can't earn money for an extended period of time. Disability insurance may seem like something you can do without, but I recommend having it unless you've built up a very healthy emergency fund. According to information on insure.com, you have a one-in-five chance of becoming disabled during your working years. You're more likely to suffer a disability than you are to die before the age of sixty-five! And when a long-term disability occurs, the average absence from work is two and a half years. That could cause a major financial strain for you or family members who depend on your income. If you don't have the option to purchase a disability policy at work (or if you do but it's not sufficient), purchase a private policy for yourself and have enough emergency money set aside to tide you over until coverage begins. Shop around at sites like disabilityquotes.com and metlife.com to get as much coverage as you can afford. There's a Disability Calculator on the MetLife site that may be helpful.

3. Life insurance is critical when your death would create a financial hardship for those you leave behind, such as a spouse or children. If you're single, or no one depends on your income, you either need a very small policy for your funeral expenses or none at all. If you have a stay-at-home spouse who cares for your children, you probably also need an adequate policy on their life to cover future child care costs. I don't recommend buying life insurance on children, because they're the ones meant to benefit from insurance proceeds. You can add a small rider to your own policy for the funeral costs of a child.

There are two basic kinds of life insurance: term and cash-value:

- **Term insurance** provides a benefit upon the death of the policy owner for a set period of time such as ten or twenty years.
- **Cash-value insurance** provides a death benefit and an investment

all wrapped up in one product. They're also called permanent life policies because you get lifetime coverage.

I prefer term insurance because it's inexpensive and provides the most death benefit for the dollar. Buying life insurance purely for investment purposes (to create a profit) defeats its purpose. As I mentioned, the reason to buy life insurance is to protect against a potential loss, not to make a gain. In most cases if you invest money in a low-cost mutual fund, instead of paying it to a life insurance company as a policy premium, you'd come out ahead.

A good rule of thumb is to purchase a policy that's ten times your income. So if you make $50,000, you might need a policy that would pay your beneficiary $500,000. But factors like the number of children you have, education expenses, mortgage payments, and the lifetime income needs of a surviving partner or spouse should come into play. If you don't have life insurance through work, or if you do but it isn't enough, take a look at the Insurance Calculators at bankrate.com to see what type of life insurance may be best for you and how much you need.

4. Auto insurance is required by most states. It's a collection of policies that protect you against financial loss. Find out the minimum requirement for your state at carinsurance.com. Rates vary depending on the kind of vehicle you have and your driving record. Choosing higher deductibles will lower your monthly premiums. You can shop auto insurance at sites like insweb.com, esurance.com, or carinsurance.com.

5. Homeowners insurance is important to protect the replacement value of your home and its contents. It's a requirement when you have a mortgage. Basic home insurance compensates you for damage to your property or contents from certain types of natural disasters, fires, and theft, for instance. You can add a rider for damage to or loss of specific expensive items like jewelry or artwork. There's also a liability portion that covers you if someone gets hurt while they're on your property. Renters also need renters insurance to cover their belongings in the event of fire or theft, for instance.

You can compare rates for these policies at homeinsurance.com or geico.com.

6. Long-term care insurance is a special type of insurance that covers many of the services you may need if you have a prolonged illness or disability that keeps you from caring for yourself on a day-to-day basis. Don't confuse it with disability insurance, which only replaces lost income. Many people mistakenly believe that they're entitled to long-term care services from their health insurance, Medicare, or Medicaid. Unfortunately, the majority of health insurance policies don't cover any long-term health care expenses. Medicare is available once you reach age sixty-five (or younger if you have certain disabilities). The requirements to qualify for Medicare are strict, and it provides medical and home health care for a limited period of time only. Find out more at medicare.gov. Medicaid is a state-administered program that may foot the bill for nursing home expenses when you have very little income and minimal financial assets. A good resource to learn more about these public programs is at the Centers for Medicare and Medicaid Web site at cms.hhs.gov.

Long-term care insurance is typically recommended for those in their fifties, but the potential for needing long-term care really exists at any age. But the older you are when you buy it, the more costly it'll be. For example, premiums can cost twice as much at age seventy than they would have at age sixty. And besides having a higher price tag, waiting to apply could result in being turned down for coverage if you're not in good health. However, buying long-term care insurance when you're younger may not be the best choice, either, because you could end up paying less-expensive premiums for a longer period of time before getting benefits, if ever. To get an idea of these costs, visit Web sites that offer free insurance quotes such as freeltcquotes.com.

7. Umbrella liability insurance may be needed as you build wealth and need additional protection. It acts like an "umbrella" that covers your underlying polices and gives you broad protection from losses above the limits of your other policies such as homeowners or auto insurance.

Having enough of the right kinds of insurance is important. Insurance won't help you build your wealth, but it certainly will help you protect it. You don't want to work so hard to buy your dream house, or save for the kind of retirement you dream of, only to lose it all with one unexpected event. If you don't already have insurance coverage, I recommend adding it to your list of goals. Review your insurance needs each year and consult with a licensed insurance professional for more information.

PLANNING FOR RETIREMENT

I said that saving for retirement is the granddaddy of all long-term goals. That's because a financially secure retirement requires a large nest egg. But planning for retirement is tricky; it's kind of like trying to plan a big party when you don't know exactly when or where it'll be, how many people will show up, or how long it will last. There are many variables to take into consideration that will surely change between now and the day you officially retire. But as fuzzy as all the variables seem right now, it's critical not to let that get in the way of getting started. Even in the face of volatile financial markets, you should never become complacent about saving for retirement.

The most important tip to successful retirement planning is simple: Start early! That's because starting earlier, rather than later, makes it possible to meet your goals on time with the greatest amount of wealth. If you accumulate a sufficient nest egg early, perhaps that sailing excursion around the world can happen at age fifty instead of at sixty-five. Or, perhaps your savings can provide needed income if you're faced with an unexpected challenge such as an illness that leaves you completely unable to work. I'm not trying to scare you into saving, but when you have an investment plan for retirement in place, there's no need to be troubled about your financial future. Also, don't worry if you haven't started saving yet; you'll just start now. With a plan in place you can live fully in the moment and stop losing sleep about your future. The best retirement plans put your investing on autopilot, and force you to pay yourself first. Automatic withdrawals from paychecks or bank accounts tend to make saving less painful because we adapt our budget to the amount of money that's left over. I'll give you some specific banking setup plans that make it easy to accomplish your goals and I'll talk more about retirement accounts like IRAs and 401(k)s in chapter 7.

But What About Social Security?

In the United States, Social Security refers to a group of benefits designed to assist eligible taxpayers. Certain programs give income to those who are retired, disabled, or survive a relative who was receiving benefits. Social Security is funded from payroll taxes—you may see it listed on your paycheck as OASDI, which stands for old-age, survivors, and disability insurance. Since you'll probably receive some amount of Social Security income in retirement, it's important to factor it into your plans.

Social Security's full retirement age has been gradually increasing because we're living longer. When Social Security benefits began in 1935, the average life expectancy was under age sixty. Workers born before 1942 were eligible to receive full Social Security benefits at age sixty-five. But for those born between the years 1943 and 1959, your full retirement age is sixty-six. And if you were born in 1960 or later, full retirement isn't available until you reach age sixty-seven. The earliest age you can start receiving Social Security retirement benefits remains sixty-two, regardless of the year you were born. However, if you elect to take Social Security retirement early, you receive benefits at a permanently reduced rate.

To qualify to receive Social Security retirement benefits, you must generally work a minimum of ten years. The calculation is based on the average of your thirty-five highest-earning years, whether you earned money in those years or not. Higher lifetime earnings result in higher benefits. The maximum benefit for a person fully retiring at age sixty-six in 2009 was $2,323 per month. Once you reach age twenty-five, Social Security statements are mailed out each year, about three months before your birthday. Remember that the statement won't include any income that didn't have Social Security taxes withheld. Review it to make sure that

Here's a quick and dirty tip: Take advantage of the online retirement planner at ssa.gov, the Social Security Web site. It's a handy way to estimate your future retirement benefits and help you plan for retirement.

your reported earnings and personal information are correct. Mistakes could keep you from receiving all the Social Security benefits you've earned. You can report errors by calling 1-800-772-1213 or by visiting a local Social Security office. Visit ssa.gov for more information.

The bottom line is that we're forced to take retirement much more seriously than those of previous generations. Everyone, young or old, must have their personalized retirement plan in place above and beyond Social Security. Many financial advisers talk about a "three-legged stool" approach to retirement that includes drawing income from (1) Social Security, (2) a workplace retirement plan savings, and (3) personal savings. I prefer to think about Social Security less as a supporting structure for future retirement income and more like gravy for the meat and potatoes of your own retirement plan. And how do you manage to provide the bulk of your retirement funds from your own savings? You guessed it: You have to start planning!

CREATE A RETIREMENT PLAN

So now you know that planning for retirement should be a long-term goal. But the big question when it comes to saving for retirement is the same question that we asked when discussing your emergency fund: How much is enough? You need to know that in order to create the plan, right? The answer is still the same: It depends on your situation. Even though many people are earning incomes from primary and secondary careers well past the typical retirement age of sixty-five, we're living longer. That's certainly a good thing, but it means that few of us will have the vigor to work up until the day we die—and who wants to do that anyway? So that means most of us should plan on providing for ourselves well past our highest income-earning years. Statistics show that if you're sixty-five, you can expect to live another fifteen years on average. And if you live to be seventy-five, you're probably going to make it to your eighty-sixth birthday! So if you want to retire early at fifty-five, you could possibly need enough savings and income to last another thirty years or more.

Don't worry, I'll show you how easy planning for retirement can be. I'll help you identify just how much you'll need to build up. All you need to do is go through the following five steps. Then you can enter your information in an online retirement calculator and let it do the complex math for you!

Step One: Assess Your Financial Needs

With so many unknowns about your future, how do you actually start to plan for retirement? We're all in the same boat when it comes to the uncertainties that relate to our future retirement. But you have to start somewhere. So the very first step in creating a retirement plan is to assess your unique financial needs. Remember that there's no right or wrong answer to questions about when you should retire or how much money you should have to do it.

The amount of annual living expenses you'll need depends entirely on what your retirement lifestyle will be like. Take some time to think realistically about what you want to do after your working years. If you envision your retirement lifestyle being very similar to the one you have now, you'll need about the same amount of income that you have now or 100 percent, adjusted for expected inflation. If you want your retirement days to be filled with lots of activities that you consider luxuries today, such as travel or other expensive hobbies, you may need more income than you have today. And if you'd like to scale down your lifestyle and enjoy a more simple existence, you may be able to do that with a smaller percentage of your current income.

We're all very different; evaluate what will make you happy. Consider what expenses you have today that you know you'll continue to have during retirement. Perhaps you'll continue to pay rent, or maybe your home mortgage will be paid off by that time. Will your food expenses be about the same, or do you envision eating out more or less during retirement? Will your clothing or dry-cleaning expenses change? Some of your expenses may decrease during your retirement. However, some of your expenses, such as medical costs or recreation, may increase in your retirement years. Depending on your health needs, you may have substantial long-term care expenses as well. Plan your potential retirement expenses conservatively, or on the high side. It's always better to plan for expenses that you never have, rather than to estimate too low and have a savings shortfall. If you're not sure what you pay annually for all your different categories of expenses, your first assignment is to measure your current expenses accurately. We're going to do that in the next section, by the way. Once you estimate what your future expenses should be, that number establishes your minimum required annual retirement income.

Step Two: Consider Your Retirement Age

After you've established the minimum annual income you believe you'll need to thrive during retirement, think about how long you're going to need that level of income. To do that you must have a retirement age in mind and an expiration date in mind. Planning for our age of death is never a pleasant task. But if you don't have a specific number in mind, I recommend being conservative and aiming high.

Your retirement age is the future age when you want to start drawing from your retirement funds. Most retirement calculators assume that after that time you won't make any additional contributions to your retirement account. So if you decide to retire at sixty-seven, then your last contribution would have been when you were age sixty-six. Multiplying minimum annual income times the number of years you'll live after you retire, gives you the total income you estimate you'll need during retirement. Yes, it's going to be a big number, and it will be even bigger after inflation is factored in.

Step Three: Consider Inflation

The rate inflation will grow between now and when you want to retire is another variable you usually must enter into a retirement calculator. Inflation is a rise in the general level of prices of goods and services over time. It must be factored into the amount you'll need for retirement because the value of your money can only be measured by its future purchasing power. As inflation causes prices to rise, every dollar buys a smaller percentage of a good or service. That's why many people, especially retirees, fear the "evils" of inflation and view it as the greatest risk to a secure financial future. We have no way of knowing the amount of inflation (or its opposite, deflation) to expect at any time in the future. The most common measure of inflation in the United States is the Consumer Price Index (CPI). We stand at about a 3 percent year-over-year inflation rate. So using a 3 percent to 4 percent inflation number for your long-term investments is a conservative estimate.

Take a look at usinflationcalculator.com, which converts any amount of money for inflation from the past into today's dollars. For example, an item that cost $1,000 in 1980 would have cost 161 percent more, $2,613, in 2009! With inflation eating away your purchasing power, it's no wonder why you have to save so much for retirement. But when you start saving early, you have more time to accumulate money and will have less stress in the planning process.

Step Four: Consider Your Return on Investment

If inflation is the evil enemy of your retirement savings, then its best friend is most certainly compounding interest! Interest you earn in most investment and bank accounts gets "compounded" when it's added back to the principal amount over and over. The result is that interest continues to be earned on an ever-growing balance. That's the closest thing to a money tree I've ever found because your money earns you more money!

The average interest rate at which your money will grow is a very important variable that you enter into a retirement calculator.

That's the annual return you expect to receive from your investments after fees and taxes. Of course, you can't predict future returns with complete certainty because the actual return for different long-term investments varies widely over time. The Standard & Poor's 500 Index or the S&P 500 (standardandpoors.com) is one of the most commonly used stock market benchmarks. It's made up of five hundred large U.S. companies with stock that's actively traded.

Consider this history for the performance of the S&P 500 over the past three decades:

- From January 1970 to January 2010, the average rate of return was approximately 12 percent.
- From January 1980 to January 2010, the average rate of return was approximately 8.7 percent.
- From January 1990 to January 2010, the average rate of return was approximately 2.4 percent.

If you isolate the returns from the past three decades and take their average, you come up with about 7 percent. Again, that is a rough estimate of potential future returns. You'll also need to consider the rate of return you'll receive after you retire—plan on it being lower than the return you earn before retirement. That's because during retirement your goal should be to preserve your wealth, to keep your nest egg extremely safe. You accomplish that by choosing conservative investments, like bank CDs and bonds, that typically earn lower rates of return than more aggressive, risky investments. Consider using a rate of return that's half of what you estimate you'll receive before retirement. For example, if you believe you can achieve an average of 6 percent growth leading up to retirement, consider using 3 percent for your estimated return during retirement.

Here's an example to consider that shows how important it is to start saving for retirement as early as you can:

If you start investing $200 per month in a mutual fund, with a 7 percent average annual return beginning at age twenty-five, you'll have over $758,000 by the time you're seventy. But if you wait until you are thirty-five to invest $200 per month at the same rate of return, you'd only have $360,000 at age seventy. That's a difference of close to $400,000 that you wouldn't have because you didn't start investing sooner, putting the magic of compounding interest to work for you.

Step Five: Start Calculating

Some of the best retirement calculators that I've found are at aarp .org and choosetosave.org. In addition to knowing your estimated retirement expenses, age to retire, life expectancy, and estimated future returns on investment, you may need to enter your estimated Social Security benefits. You can use the benefits calculator at ssa .gov to get that information.

Below is information I entered into the Retirement Nest Egg Calculator at aarp.org for Mark, who's twenty-eight and currently single. I made the assumption that he'll work until he's sixty-seven years old and then will need retirement income for twenty-three years until he's ninety. He's only got $1,000 saved for retirement, but plans to start investing in his workplace retirement plan right away. There's a stock fund in the plan menu with a ten-year average return of 7 percent. He believes that he could be satisfied with 90 percent of his current income in retirement.

Current age:	28
Age of retirement:	67
Household income:	$40,000
Current retirement savings:	$1,000
Rate of return before retirement:	7%
Rate of return during retirement:	4%
Years of retirement income:	23
Percent of income at retirement:	90%
Expected salary increase:	3%
Expected rate of inflation:	3%
Include Social Security income:	yes

Based on the above information, the calculator estimates that Mark's nest egg needs to be $1,425,464, which takes his projected Social Security income at age sixty-seven into account. The calculator shows that in order for Mark to have that much money to draw from, he'll need to put $682 per month toward his retirement fund. You can play with calculator variables to see how they affect the amount you need to save. For instance, if Mark waited until seventy to retire and chose an investment with an 8 percent return instead of a 7 percent return, he'd need to save $370 per month.

Remember that a retirement calculator is a tool that can't estimate every factor of your unique circumstances. For instance, if you currently have expensive medical needs or a family history that indicates you may have such challenges in the future, it would be wise to save more than what a retirement calculator indicates. I've found that no two retirement calculators ask for the same input data or give you the same results, so try using a couple of them to compare various outcomes. The information should be used to help you approximate how much to set aside each month for your future. However, this is merely your starting point because you're going to update your retirement plan on a regular basis going forward. Retirement planning is not a set-it-and-forget-it process. It must be an evergreen, flexible action plan that you adjust as you age and change. You will fine-tune the plan every year or so to make it come into focus a bit more each time you review it.

If you don't want to do any calculating and prefer to leave all your retirement planning up to a professional, I recommend using a certified financial planner (CFP). You'll want to find someone you feel comfortable talking to who's willing to offer credible solutions and work toward your best interests. You may find good referrals from friends, business associates, or the National Association of Personal Financial Advisors Web site at napfa.org.

The final step in your planning is to just do it. There are some special types of retirement accounts for individuals, employees, and the self-employed that are designed to help you reach your goal faster. I'll show you how to open your retirement account(s) and

Here's a quick and dirty tip: Add "Review my retirement plan" to your list of New Year's resolutions every year until the time you decide to pull the trigger on your retirement!

pick your investments in chapter 7. But first, let's figure out how to start saving for your future.

CREATE A SPENDING PLAN THAT WILL WORK

After you get a clear picture of where your personal finances stand today (by creating your Personal Financial Statement) and where you'd like them to be (by setting realistic financial goals), the next step is to close the gap between the two. The best way to do that is to understand where your money goes. After you dig into your cash flow, you'll clearly see your spending problems and be able to reprioritize expenses. That's how you make room for the money you need to put aside for your short-, medium-, and long-term goals.

I'll admit that budgeting isn't something I like to do. I think many of us shudder at the word *budget* because it implies doing without the things we want—kind of like dieting. But I do like spending! Creating a "spending plan" just sounds so much better than creating a budget. A spending plan is simply a plan for how you intend to manage your money. The goal in creating one is to make sure you account for your financial goals in addition to all your living expenses. You'll define all your monthly expenses by broad categories and assign them an allowable percentage of your monthly income. The total of all your expenses must balance with, or zero out, your take-home income. As you monitor your spending, you can adjust your expenses as needed, and make sure you have enough discretionary money left over to accomplish your goals. I'll give you some examples in the next section.

And here's the good news: I'm not going to tell you what percentage of your income should be allocated to groceries or entertainment, for example. That's because you have unique priorities that may be very different from mine. You may enjoy dining out a couple nights a week so much, that you're willing to delay saving for the purchase of a new car. Or you may resist buying new clothes for a year in order to take a vacation. It's all up to you to decide how your financial resources should be spent. A big part of creating your spending plan is putting your priorities into perspective. That should give you the motivation to carry it out on a daily basis. Will you slip up occasionally and buy something that wasn't in the plan or pay more for something than you anticipated? Absolutely. The car will need a repair that you didn't expect. Your family may need some help from you. There are a million ways you can get temporarily derailed from a spending plan.

The goal of a spending plan is not to make you miserable. Its implementation should get you excited, because what's truly important to you is being accounted for and addressed in the plan. You don't have to fear that you're not allocating enough money to your children's education fund when it's part of your spending plan. You won't have to worry about your retirement savings, either. In fact, you may get so excited about saving for the things you really want, that you'll enjoy sacrificing spending on what doesn't matter to you. It can become a game for some people who really get fired-up about seeing their goals become a reality!

So let's get started by creating a spending plan that'll work for you. I recommend that you enter data in a computer spreadsheet or financial program (which I'll discuss more in chapter 4), but writing it down on paper works, too. The first task is to estimate your monthly after-tax income. For some this is easy because you receive a regular paycheck. For others who are paid on commission or who are self-employed, you'll need to come up with a realistic monthly income estimate.

The second task is to enter all of your fixed monthly expenses below your income. Fixed expenses, such as rent, a mortgage, or a car payment, are those recurring costs that you must pay every month because they're vital for your well-being or are commitments you've already made. Label each category or payment on a separate row. Don't forget to account for any automatic payroll deductions you may have for workplace insurance or a retirement plan. Some fixed expenses you don't actually pay for in equal amounts each month,

Here's a quick and dirty tip: Many utility companies offer a budget billing option, which allows you to pay an equal amount each month. That can be helpful if you live in an area with extreme climate changes.

so come up with a monthly average. For instance, if you pay insurance just twice a year, calculate the annual amount you pay, and then divide by 12. Or if your utility bills fluctuate a lot, research the total you paid for a full twelve-month period and divide by 12.

The third task is to enter all your variable monthly expenses below your fixed expenses. Variable expenses are those that can change each month or are discretionary. Dining out, buying clothes, groceries, or getting a haircut could be some of your variable expense categories. Try to think of all the ways you spend money. Maybe going to the movies or to a local coffee shop are black holes for your money. If so, be sure to create separate categories just for them. Enter the average of your actual expenses from at least three previous months by looking at charges on your account statements. If you don't have these, you'll simply need to start tracking your expenses going forward.

Your spending strategy should be based on your historical spending patterns. You need to analyze your most recent spending in order to plan your future spending. Once you have at least a few months of historical income and expenses accurately recorded, your next task is to create new spending guidelines for yourself. Decide how much you'd like to save each month and then decide where to cut back. You have many needs and wants that are all competing for your limited resources. You have to decide the best way to balance your current expenses and savings needs so you never spend more than you make.

Here's a quick and dirty tip: PearBudget.com is an elegant online budgeting tool you can use to enter your actual income and expenses to compare against your proposed budget. Try it for free for thirty days, then the service charges $3 per month.

Remember Mark from the retirement planning section? Let's take a look at his household spending before and after his financial planning:

MARK'S MONTHLY SPENDING BEFORE HAVING A FINANCIAL PLAN		
CATEGORY	AMOUNT	PERCENTAGE
TOTAL AFTER-TAX INCOME	$2,565	100%
Rent	$700	27%
Utilities	$130	5%
Car loan	$350	14%
Insurance	$75	3%
Groceries	$525	20%
Restaurants	$125	5%
Clothing	$200	8%
Entertainment	$300	12%
Other	$160	6%
TOTAL EXPENSES	$2,565	100%

If Mark decided to save $370 each month to meet his long-term goal to retire at age seventy, he'd enter that amount as a fixed monthly expense on his spending plan. He also has a short-term goal to build up at least $1,200 for his emergency fund within a year—so that's a minimum of $100 per month. Here's what his spending plan looks like after including his goals and deciding to cut back in several categories such as restaurants, clothing, and entertainment:

MARK'S MONTHLY SPENDING PLAN		
CATEGORY	AMOUNT	PERCENTAGE
TOTAL AFTER-TAX INCOME	$2,565	100%
Rent	$700	27%
Utilities	$130	5%
Car loan	$350	14%
Insurance	$75	3%
Retirement fund	**$370**	**14%**
Emergency fund	**$100**	**4%**
Groceries	$500	19%
Restaurants	$75	3%
Clothing	$100	4%
Entertainment	$90	4%
Other	$75	3%
TOTAL EXPENSES	$2,565	100%

Enter the amounts you need to save or invest to accomplish your short-, medium-, and long-term goals in your spending plan. Then cut back spending in every category you can to make your savings and investments a top priority. There are a couple of different ways to approach it. You can cut all of your variable expenses across the board by 15 percent, for example. Or, you can pick and choose some categories to really cut back and leave the others alone—that's what Mark did. Take a hard look at which expenses you can reduce or eliminate right away. Establish the monetary amounts or percentages for an ideal or model month. For example, if over the past few months you've spent 5 percent of your after-tax income on entertainment, perhaps that amount could be reduced to 3 percent. Or if you've spent an average of $400 a month dining out, maybe you could limit it to $300 going forward. You have to set your own priorities about which expenses you're willing to reduce.

Here's a quick and dirty tip: Use the Savings Goal Calculator in the checking and savings section at bankrate.com to figure the monthly, weekly, or daily amount you need to set aside for your financial goals.

The great news is that you can reanalyze and reprioritize your situation at any time. When your actual spending deviates from your ideal spending plan, it's time to regroup and move forward. That's how progress is made, month by month, and year by year. The important point is that you're aware of your financial progress, or lack of it, instead of sticking your head in the sand about it. No matter what your time horizon, the key to making a goal happen is to enter its monthly cost on your spending plan. If you can't afford it right now, you'll have some tough decisions to make about what you should bump off your spending plan. That's where the rubber meets the road and you truly rank your priorities. When you save for emergencies and invest wisely for retirement, you're actually choosing to purchase a happy and secure financial future instead of buying something that may be unnecessary and quickly forgotten.

Increase Your Discretionary Income

When you subtract your monthly fixed and variable expenses from your monthly after-tax income, what you have left over is your discretionary income. The obvious goal is to grow your discretionary income and to make saving a priority over spending. Consider anything you can do to increase your income and decrease your expenses.

Make a commitment to yourself to become your own spending detective. If you can carefully track your expenses, you'll probably be amazed at the ways you can plug unnecessary spending leaks and save money. Whether you track expenses manually or electronically, the goal is to be as thorough as possible. Make sure that each and every check you write, charge you make to a debit or credit card, and cash amount you dole out is recorded.

Here's a quick and dirty tip: Billshrink.com is a free savings tool that makes personalized recommendations to save you money on mobile phone plans, credit cards, and gasoline purchases, based on your actual everyday usage.

Some of the many benefits of using money management software or online financial applications are their helpful planning and budgeting functions. In the computer money management section in chapter 4, I'll detail different programs and tools that can make money management and budget tracking easy, and (maybe) even fun!

Your job is to find a way to track your cash inflows and outflows that works best for you. Once you've used your spending plan to cut expenses and maximize your discretionary income, you'll want to put that money to work for you.

Spending Plan Summary

There are three basic steps to implementing your spending plan:

1. Identify how you're spending money now by tracking at least three months of your most recent expenses.
2. Evaluate your spending and redesign it so you have enough money left over to save and invest for your goals.
3. Track your spending each month so you know if you're spending within the limits you set for yourself. When you spend too much, cut back in the categories that are easiest for you. If you still can't meet your guidelines, you'll need to make tougher spending sacrifices.

15 WAYS TO SAVE MORE MONEY

There are lots of ways to stay on track with your model spending strategy. Here are fifteen tips for how to save more money:

1. **Evaluate your housing situation.** Is there a way to pay less? Perhaps renting a larger home or apartment would allow you to have a roommate or two to share expenses and come out ahead. Or consider if buying a home could be more economical for you in the long run. If you buy at the right price, it's possible that home ownership may be less expensive than renting. If you already own a home, you'll learn strategies in chapter 5 to reduce your mortgage liability, such as refinancing or doing a loan modification. Chapter 8 will tell you everything you need to know about buying real estate and if it's the right move for you.

2. **Reduce your power bills.** Your electric heating and air-conditioning system sucks up most of the power that you pay for. When it's warm, every degree you choose to raise the thermostat above seventy-eight can reduce your cooling costs by as much as 10 percent. And in winter, every degree you warm your home above seventy can cost you an additional 7 percent to 10 percent. Portable fans or ceiling fans are inexpensive and allow most people to raise their thermostat in warm weather by approximately three to four degrees and feel just as comfortable. Just be sure to turn off the fans when you leave the room. Remember that anything plugged into electric sockets is pulling some electricity. So unplug electric chargers and appliances that don't need to stay on all the time, like coffee machines. Clothes dryers pull a lot of energy, so remove clothes while they're still slightly damp and do one dryer load right after another to maximize the built-up heat from the prior load. Visit your power company's Web site to find out more about inspections, energy-saving tips for your geographic area, and budget billing that may allow you to pay a fixed amount each month based on your historical power usage.

3. **Be smart with your water use.** Consider installing inexpensive water flow regulators in showers and opting for shorter laundry cycles that use more cold water. You can also reduce your hot-water heater setting. For every ten degrees that you reduce it, it's possible to lower your power bill by 5 percent. A good water temperature is

120 degrees if your dishwasher has a hot water booster, or 130 degrees if not. For more money-saving tips, take a look at these two Web sites: the American Council for an Energy-Efficient Economy at aceee.org and the U.S. Department of Energy's site devoted to energy efficiency and renewable energy at eere.energy.gov.

4. Slim down your household expenses. Are you in the habit of paying bills for your telephone, television, cell phone, and Internet without scrutinizing them or seriously shopping around for better deals? Look at your options for lower-priced packages that bundle those services. Consider ditching your telephone landline and going totally cellular! I haven't had a landline for years and it hasn't posed a problem yet. It'll save you money and put an end to those dinner-disturbing sales calls. Compare cell phone plans at myrateplan.com.

5. Cook with a microwave oven when you can. They're inexpensive and use up to 30 percent less energy than a traditional oven. Plus, they don't generate heat in the kitchen during warm weather.

6. Eliminate banking fees. You should never have to pay banking expenses related to ATMs, paper checks, and overdraft, statement, and transaction fees. The next chapter will get you up to speed on how to get the most out of your banking accounts.

7. Reduce your payroll tax withholding. Many people have too much federal taxes withheld from their paychecks. If you're in that boat, it's much better to receive a higher paycheck now so you can save more money, than to wait and receive the excess withholding as a tax refund many months in the future. Ask your employer for a Form W-4 or download it from the Internal Revenue Service (IRS) Web site at irs.gov so you can revise it and get an instant pay raise.

8. Raise your insurance deductibles. The higher your deductibles, the lower your insurance payments will be. Review all your policies, such as homeowners, auto, and health, at least once a year to make sure you have the best deal. Sit down with an insurance agent or go to insweb.com to see where you can cut back but still have adequate coverage. Shop around at sites like ehealthinsurance .com to see if you can beat the health insurance you get through work. One benefit to having your own health insurance is that you'll maintain coverage if you tend to change jobs frequently. You may opt for a high-deductible plan with lower premiums and the unique ability to save money for health care expenses in a tax-advantaged health savings account (HSA).

9. **Use a Flexible Savings Arrangement (FSA).** If your employer offers an FSA, you can have money deducted on a pre-tax basis to pay for health and child care costs. That saves you money on expenses you'd have to pay for anyway. Estimate how much you want to save carefully, however, because if you don't spend the full amount deducted from your paycheck by an annual deadline, you lose it. (With an HSA, your contributions stay in the account indefinitely—there's no penalty if you don't use the money each year.)

10. **Get free media and entertainment.** Remember the library? Stuff is free there like books, DVDs, and Internet service. You could also cancel your paid television service completely—digital channels are free. You can even watch many shows 24/7 on the Web at sites like hulu.com. I'm a huge fan of free podcasts—who needs to pay for satellite radio when you can download national or independent news and entertainment shows for free?

11. **Cook at home and stay healthy.** Make a commitment to eat right, exercise, and quit smoking. Good health can save you lots of money on doctor bills, medication, and maybe even make you eligible for preferred rates on health, life, and disability insurance. Cooking at home is inexpensive and allows you to make wise food choices. Try using a meal plan service like e-mealz.com that creates your dinner menu for a week. You receive a customized, one-page plan with a complete grocery list based on the weekly sales at the store(s) you choose to shop, like Publix, Walmart, or ALDI. Your

total grocery bill for a week's worth of dinners for four to six people will average about $75.

12. **Don't pay full price.** Sometimes saving money just means buying smarter. Find great coupons, savings offers, and freebies at sites like:

- coupons.com
- redplum.com
- smartsource.com
- befrugal.com
- retailmenot.com
- wisebread.com
- eatbetteramerica.com (funded by General Mills)
- pgeverydaysolutions.com (funded by Proctor & Gamble)

The Internet makes it easy to shop and compare prices. I love buying nonperishable products in bulk from amazon.com and having them delivered to my front door.

Visit Web sites of the grocery and pharmacy stores where you shop, like publix.com, albertsons.com, aldi.com, walmart.com, target .com, walgreens.com, and cvs.com for special offers and coupons. You can come out ahead by joining local discount superstores like Costco, Sam's Club, or BJ's Wholesale, even after paying the annual membership fee. If you don't have storage space to buy in bulk, shop with a friend or neighbor and split your bulk purchases.

13. **Eat out the smart way.** If you're like me and enjoy eating out (a lot!), you can save money by choosing restaurants that are reasonably priced and offer large portion sizes. I'm a big fan of getting two or more meals out of one by taking home leftovers or getting takeout. Go to restaurants that don't employ waitstaff, but serve you from a pick-up counter instead because that eliminates having to tip a server. Also, limit your alcoholic beverages in restaurants to special occasions. Most establishments make a killing on beer, wine, and cocktails, so opt for water, which is inexpensive and healthy, too.

14. **Choose energy-efficient appliances and vehicles.** When you need to replace an old appliance or buy a newer car, consider energy-efficient models that can save you power, water, or gasoline, and are good for the environment. They may cost a little more up front, but if you keep them long enough, they'll usually save you money. Some purchases may qualify for federal or state tax credits or certain rebates. Go to energystar.gov for more information.

15. **Maintain what you have.** Your vehicles, air-conditioning system, water heater, clothes washer and dryer, or anything else you own that uses energy, requires regular maintenance to extend its life and run efficiently. And once a vehicle is paid for, try to keep it as long as possible. When repairs are needed, remind yourself how those costs stack up against the monthly payments you used to make. Also, try not to buy things that require a lot of maintenance in the first place.

3

Choosing the Best Banking Accounts

> I don't have a bank account, because I don't
> know my mother's maiden name.
>
> —PAULA POUNDSTONE, comedienne

I hope you're ready to conquer the world now that you know your financial goals and have a spending strategy to get you there! With all the extra discretionary money you're going to create, you need to make sure you're putting it in the right banking accounts. Then in chapter 4 we'll make sure that you manage it the best way possible.

Choosing the best bank accounts is a smart and important move because the banks you select will pay you competitive rates of interest and also lay the foundation for your entire money management system. Having the right credit accounts are important, too, so you don't pay excessive interest and fees to banks and other lending institutions. We'll cover more on credit cards in chapter 5, which is about dealing with debt. In the next section we'll go into more detail about each of the most common bank account types for individuals and families. Once you understand their pros and cons you'll understand how they can best fit into your overall money management strategy.

DIFFERENT TYPES OF BANK ACCOUNTS

There are four basic types of bank accounts:

1. Checking accounts
2. Savings accounts
3. Money market deposit accounts (MMDAs)
4. Certificates of deposit (CDs)

The first three are demand deposit accounts. That means you can demand, or withdraw, your money at any time without giving notice to the bank or incurring a penalty. Checking, savings, and money markets pay a variable rate of interest that's subject to change or to certain account terms and conditions. The fourth type, a CD, is a time deposit account. That means you're required to leave your money in the account for a specified period of time, such as a month or five years. In return for the use of your money, the financial institution pays you a fixed rate of interest.

Which type of account you need is largely determined by how you'll use your money. Checking accounts are perfect for money that you access on a daily basis; savings and money markets work well for funds that you don't need to withdraw more than a few times a month; and CDs are for money that you don't need to touch for some time. We'll get into more detail on how each of these accounts work. But an important consideration for choosing an account is the amount of interest it pays—its yield.

There's no set rule for how much money you should keep in different types of bank accounts. My strategy is to keep or move as much money as possible into the highest-yielding account that I have or can find. For instance, if I can earn 2 percent interest from my online savings account and 0.15 percent from my checking

Here's a quick and dirty tip: Always compare annual percentage yield or APY of different bank account offers to make sure you're comparing interest rates fairly.

account, I'd rather move any excess money in my checking into my online savings. That allows me to maximize my interest earnings. The interest rates you receive on your bank accounts will depend on various factors, such as how much money you have and whether you have multiple accounts with the same institution, for example. Money markets are generally more beneficial than savings accounts when you have more money to deposit. If your checking account receives little or no interest, you should only keep enough money in the account to cover your monthly bills and spending (or find a high-yield checking account—I'll show you one in the next section!). The excess can be transferred to another account that will maximize your interest income. Always look for ways to earn the highest interest on money that you don't need for your short-term transactions.

CHECKING OR PAYMENT ACCOUNTS

A checking account is the most useful tool for day-to-day spending, paying bills, and for depositing funds. As the use of paper checks becomes less common, they're beginning to be called "payment accounts" instead. No matter what it's called, it's a workhorse that none of us should be without. Your checking account should charge no fees, require no minimum balance, and should offer unlimited use of checks, debit card charges, telephone banking, online banking, and automatic teller machines (ATMs). Checking/payment accounts are extremely liquid because you can deposit, withdraw, or transfer any amount of money any number of times. Because they offer so much flexibility and convenience, they've traditionally paid the least amount of interest when compared to other account types. However, times are changing. There are hundreds of community banks paying impressive interest rates if you just know where to find them. But you can't let the fact that their nearest branch might be 1,000 miles away hold you back. The perks usually come with more rules or requirements than regular checking accounts, but they're well worth it. Here's an example at the time of writing*:

---

* Please remember that this is just an example. Offers are constantly changing and by the time you are reading this book, this offer may no longer exist, or there might be even

The Bank of the Sierra was founded in 1977 and has more than twenty-five branches in California. Their Reward Checking is a free, high-interest account with no minimum balance—it just requires $50 to open an account. They currently pay 4.09% APY on the portion of your balance that's less than $25,000 and 1.01% APY on the portion of your balance that exceeds $25,000. Those rates have been in effect since December 2009. The account comes with a free debit card, free online banking, and free bill pay. They also reimburse up to $25 in foreign ATM fees nationwide per month. Here are the requirements you must meet each statement cycle:

- Make a minimum of 12 debit-card purchases (ATM usage doesn't count)
- Make one automatic payment or direct deposit
- Receive your monthly statement electronically
- Make one payment using Bill Pay

If you don't meet the qualifications, your interest rate for the statement cycle is dropped to 0.12% APY and you don't get an $25 ATM reimbursement—but there are no penalties.

For many of you, these four requirements would be easy because you're already doing them! And if you aren't, it's simple to make a change like receiving a statement online instead of in the mail, or to set up one of your recurring bills for an automatic payment. But this isn't an advertisement for that bank, it's just an illustration of the kinds of good banking deals that are out there. Most traditional checking accounts offer zero interest or perhaps less than 0.25 percent. If you were able to move $10,000 of your money from a savings account that earns 1 percent, into this high-yield checking account, you'd earn an additional 3.3 percent on your money. That's $330 more in your pocket each year.

So the idea is to be proactive about searching for the best offers on a regular basis. But remember that when you take advantage of

---

better offers out there. This example is intended to show the kinds of great offers that exist.

> Here's a quick and dirty tip: When you have to make a certain number of debit transactions per statement cycle, put a sticky note on the back of your debit card to list the date of your purchases. That way you'll be sure to reach the required minimum before the cut-off date.

a great checking or savings offer, the interest rate can decrease at any time because it's a variable rate (as opposed to a fixed rate that CDs typically provide). That means the rate may quietly creep down to a less competitive rate without you realizing it. Keep tabs on the best checking/payment accounts by visiting checkingfinder .com.

WHAT HAPPENS IF YOUR DEBIT CARD IS LOST OR STOLEN?

If your debit card is ever lost or stolen, be sure to report your loss immediately. Your potential liability for the loss of a debit card depends on how quickly you notify the bank as follows:

- Report a loss before any misuse occurs: your liability is $0
- Report a loss within two business days: your maximum liability is $50
- Report a loss within sixty days of receiving your account statement showing the misuse: your maximum liability is $500
- Report a loss after sixty days of receiving your account statement showing the misuse: your liability is unlimited. You could lose all the money in the account, plus have to pay penalty fees.

Having a savings or money market deposit account, in addition to your checking account, at the same institution may be beneficial. The additional account can help you qualify for a preferred checking/payment account, depending on the total balance of all your accounts. Preferred accounts can offer benefits such as a higher interest rate, free checks, free debit cards, free use of another bank's ATM, and overdraft protection. Overdraft happens if you accidentally write a check or make a debit card charge that exceeds your current checking balance. The shortage can be covered by an automatic draft from your other account, which can save you big bucks on potential fees and penalties.

Differences Between Online and Regular Accounts

If you've never had an account at an online bank, it may seem a little strange not to be able to go to a branch to withdraw money or to make a deposit. You can usually do both of those for free by using an ATM that's in the online bank's network. And if you have to go outside of the network, many banks will reimburse you for a certain number of ATM fees that you incur. Additionally, most online banks are FDIC-insured (more about that is coming up). So there's no reason not to consider online banks and search out a better offer. But if you still want to use the services of a local bank, you can always keep a checking account at one. That's what I do, mainly for the convenience of depositing paper checks. For money that I want to save, I transfer it from my checking into a high-interest online savings account. And if I need to access my savings, I simply transfer money back into my checking account without paying any fees. Funds in online savings accounts can usually only be accessed by electronic transfer; however, there are some that offer check cards.

Consider Online Banking and Bill Pay

If you want to dramatically simplify paying your bills, make sure to select a checking/payment account that offers free online banking

---

Here's a quick and dirty tip: Use the power of the Internet to find the best bank account offers. Sites like checkingfinder.com, money-rates. com, and bankrate.com are always gathering information for you about the best deals!

and bill pay. If you're not familiar with paying bills online, it can revolutionize the way you send payments to companies and individuals. I was so pleasantly surprised to find that I never had to buy checks, print checks, lick envelopes, or keep a large supply of postage stamps ever again! Online bill pay allows you to pay anyone in the United States that you would normally pay by check or automatic debit.

If your utility or insurance companies, for example, are linked with online bill pay services, you can elect to receive e-bills directly in your online payment center. Or you can enter bills manually as they arrive by mail, e-mail, or when you need to send anyone a check. To enter a bill, you type in the payment amount and the date you want the payment to be received by the company or individual. For bills that can be paid electronically, perhaps for your power bill or mortgage, for example, the payment can be transferred electronically the same or next business day. For a payment to someone who requires a check, such as a friend or a local handyman, they're mailed to the billing address you enter and usually arrive in about four days. Most online bill pay systems show you a calendar with the earliest business date that they can deliver your payment to a person or company. You can accept this date or change it to a later one that's not more than a year into the future. Paying bills from one place, such as your bank's Web site, really beats paying bills from multiple vendor sites.

Here are some common online bill pay features and advantages that many banks offer:

- View a summary of pending payments by due date
- Get a history of payments already made
- Receive e-bills instead of paper bills in the mail
- Set up automatic bill payments
- Schedule recurring payments to go out at regular intervals
- Export payment information to desktop software
- Receive e-mail alerts and reminders when bills are due or paid
- Make payments from multiple bank accounts
- Easily make changes to or cancel pending payments

Here's a quick and dirty tip: USAA at usaa.com offers banking services with an application for the iPhone that allows you to instantly deposit checks from anywhere by simply taking a picture of it.

SAVINGS ACCOUNTS

A savings account generally doesn't have the flexibility of a checking/payment account, but is designed to keep funds safe and generate modest interest. Savings accounts usually limit the number of withdrawals that can be made per statement cycle. Checks and debit cards are usually not issued with a true savings account; however, some may offer an ATM card. Transfers from savings to other accounts can be made in local branches or exclusively online. Even with these slight restrictions, a savings account is still one of the most liquid account types you can have and is perfect for your short-term savings goals. For example, you could have one savings account for the down payment on the new car that you want to buy before the end of the year, and another for your holiday gift-giving fund. But for large amounts of money or for more payment flexibility, consider saving in a money market deposit account.

Interest rates on savings accounts vary, so it's important to shop around. And as I mentioned, the rate on each account is variable, so it can decrease after you open the account. Some of the best interest rates that I've found pay up to 2 percent interest.

MONEY MARKET DEPOSIT ACCOUNTS (MMDAs)

A money market deposit account is a type of savings account that offers more flexibility than a regular savings account, but less than a checking/payment account. It may also offer a higher rate of interest for keeping a large minimum balance. It's a favorite of mine because it combines some of the features of both checking and savings accounts. You can make payments with checks, debit cards, ATMs, and using online banking. With MMDAs, withdrawals are restricted to six per statement cycle and no more than three of those can be by check. The increased payment flexibility along with higher interest income makes the MMDA a great choice for emergency reserve funds or money that you don't plan on needing very often. As with savings accounts, the interest rates on MMDAs vary, so shop around locally and online for the best offers. The highest rates right now approach 2 percent and vary depending on how much you deposit.

CERTIFICATES OF DEPOSIT (CDs)

As I mentioned, a certificate of deposit is a type of bank account that's called a time deposit. They entitle the holder to receive a fixed amount of interest for a specific period of time. You generally have to keep a CD deposit in the bank until the end of the period, which is called the maturity date. Higher rates of interest are offered in exchange for keeping larger amounts of money on deposit for longer terms. For example, a six-month CD may pay 1.5 percent interest and a five-year CD may pay 3.25 percent. Some of the highest rates are for "jumbo CDs" that require a minimum deposit of $100,000. That makes them a good option when you have a large amount of money that you want to keep very safe and don't need to spend. But you'll need to shop CDs carefully because the terms and interest rates vary.

Most institutions allow you to receive CD interest income either monthly or semiannually as a check or as a transfer into another account. If you're using a CD as a long-term savings vehicle, opt to have the interest income reinvested, unless you can earn a better return in another investment. Withdrawing any amount of the principal from a traditional CD before the maturity date usually triggers an early withdrawal penalty. So before depositing money in a CD, be sure that you fully understand all its terms and that you can do without the money for the duration of the term. A high interest rate can be wiped out if you find yourself in a cash crunch and have to pay a steep penalty for an early withdrawal from a CD.

Where to Put Your Money: An Example

If you still aren't sure exactly where to put your money, let's take a look at how Joanna uses three different types of banking accounts to her advantage:

Joanna manages a dental office and contributes 10 percent of her paycheck to her workplace retirement plan. She's done a great job saving money over the years and always keeps $10,000 in her emergency fund, which is six months' worth of her living expenses. She opened a money market deposit account that earns 2 percent APY with a free debit card and paper checks. She rarely needs to access her emergency money, but last year she did have an unexpected car repair that was over $1,000 and it was easy to pay the bill using her money market debit card.

At the end of each year Joanna earns a bonus. She likes to put her annual bonus payments in a five-year CD. That's money that she can't touch for five years without penalty. But since she feels that her job is secure and that having $10,000 is enough of a safety net, she likes earning a higher return on her bonus money. The $2,000 CD she opened last year is earning 3.5 percent—and the one she opened the prior year is earning 4 percent.

The third type of bank account that Joanna uses is an online checking account that she found at checkingfinder.com. She uses it to pay for all her household bills, like rent and utilities, and for her everyday spending on items like groceries and gas. She usually has just enough money in the account to cover her expenses. The checking account has free online banking, a free debit card, no minimum balance requirement, and a free introductory package of fifty paper checks. It also pays 2 percent on balances up to $25,000 with some restrictions. She has to (1) make a minimum of ten purchases from the account using the debit card each month, (2) receive an electronic statement, (3) have either one direct deposit or an automatic payment transfer each month, and (4) sign on to her online banking account at least once each month. She's more than happy to comply with those requirements to earn interest on the money in her checking. Her old checking account didn't pay any interest and charged her a monthly service fee.

TRUST ACCOUNTS

When you want to deposit money in any type of bank account that will eventually go to someone else—such as a family member or friend—after your death, you create a trust account. The account owner is called the trustee and the person who will receive the money upon the account owner's death is called the beneficiary. There are revocable trust accounts that provide the flexibility to be changed, and irrevocable trust accounts that cannot be modified without the permission of the beneficiary.

Revocable trusts are the most common type and they're also known as payable on death (POD) accounts, in trust for (ITF) accounts, and Totten trust accounts. The account owner simply signs an agreement stating that the deposits will be payable to one or more beneficiaries upon their death. A beneficiary must be a family member, nonfamily member, charity, or other IRS-recognized nonprofit organization to be eligible for FDIC insurance.

FEDERAL DEPOSIT INSURANCE CORPORATION (FDIC) INSURANCE

An important requirement for the four account types that we've discussed is that they have FDIC insurance. The FDIC was established in 1933 to protect consumers from bank failures. They proudly state that not one penny of insured funds has ever been lost since their inception. Choosing to put your money in accounts at FDIC-insured institutions (whether they're local or online) is mandatory, in my opinion. However, there seems to be a lot of confusion about FDIC insurance. After the start of the financial crisis of 2008, I got a steady stream of e-mails from *Money Girl* podcast listeners and blog readers who were panicked about whether their funds would be protected by the FDIC. They saw bank failures on television and wondered if their institution would be the next one to collapse.

Many people are unclear about what types of accounts are insured and for how much. Let's be sure you understand how FDIC insurance works so you can be fully protected.

The current FDIC insurance limits were increased in October 2008. Congress bumped them up from $100,000 to $250,000 per depositor and in 2010 made these increased limits permanent. Here are the FDIC deposit insurance coverage limits:

OWNERSHIP TYPE	FDIC COVERAGE LIMITS
Single Accounts (owned by one person)	$250,000 per owner
Joint Accounts (owned by two more people)	$250,000 per co-owner
Certain Retirement Accounts (always owned by one person)	$250,000 per owner
Trust Accounts (can be owned by one or more people)	$250,000 per owner per beneficiary (subject to limitations)
Corporation, Partnership and Unincorporated Association Accounts	$250,000 per entity
Employee Benefit Plan Accounts	$250,000 per participant
Government Accounts	$250,000 per custodian

The FDIC provides separate coverage for each of the seven ownership types listed in the chart above. For individuals and families, the most important ones are the first four: single, joint, retirement, and trusts. The coverage amounts listed refer to the total of all deposits held in that ownership type at a unique FDIC-insured bank. You can own any of the four bank account types that we've just covered (checking, savings, MMDAs, and CDs) as a single person or jointly,

Here's a quick and dirty tip: Find which banks are FDIC-insured at fdic.gov, using the Bank Find look-up tool. You can type in your online bank, local bank, or even just your zip code to see which institutions offer FDIC insurance to depositors.

as a coowner with one or more people. You can also set up your bank accounts as trust accounts or retirement accounts.

The FDIC does not insure the contents of safe-deposit boxes, nor do they insure stolen funds. They don't insure any investment product or account that holds stocks, bonds, mutual funds, life insurance policies, treasuries, annuities, or money market mutual funds. FDIC insurance can be a little confusing, but if you understand the rules I've presented and apply them to your bank accounts, you'll never have to worry about being the victim of a bank failure.

What if You're Above the FDIC Limits?

If you ever find yourself above the allowable FDIC insurance limits, speak with a personal banker about your situation. Certain banks offer special FDIC insurance to cover high deposit customers so they don't have to take a portion of their deposits to other institutions. It's called the Certificate of Deposit Account Registry Service or CDARS. It gives full FDIC insurance on deposits of up to $50 million. The customer, which may be an individual, a business, or a nonprofit organization, must sign an agreement with the participating institution. Find out more and locate thousands of institutions in the United States that offer CDARS at cdars.com.

Here's a quick and dirty tip: Deposits held at most credit unions are insured by the National Credit Union Administration (NCUA) with limits that match FDIC insurance. Find out more at ncua.gov.

4

Setting Up a Money Management System

> The Internet is the most important single development in the history of human communication since the invention of call waiting.
>
> —DAVE BARRY, author

After you've created a realistic spending plan and have the right accounts set up for all your banking needs, you'll want to establish a money management system. A money management system is the way you handle all your personal finances, such as categorizing everyday expenses, paying your bills, filing necessary documents, and monitoring your investments. It's simply a set of tasks that you accomplish on a consistent basis to help you achieve your financial goals. The purpose of your system is to keep you organized so nothing important slips through the cracks. Having a neat money management system will increase the likelihood that you'll make great financial strides year after year. The trick is to establish a routine and to maintain the habits to make it work. Without the right habits, a system will always fall apart.

I have good news if you feel financially overwhelmed or unqualified to manage your money: Technology can come to your rescue. In this chapter, I'll show you how to set up a computerized system that'll make your life easier. You'll get your bills paid on time, categorize your everyday expenses quickly, easily reconcile your accounts, and get ready for tax day with less stress. My personal requirement for a money management system is that it's comprehensive but easy. I'm going to share my system with you so you can copy it or use it as a starting point to create your own.

REGULAR MONEY MANAGEMENT TASKS

The following are the most important money management tasks that you need to accomplish on a routine basis:

MONEY MANAGEMENT TASK	SCHEDULE TO COMPLETE
Pay bills on time	Weekly
Categorize deposits, checks, debit card charges, withdrawals, credit card charges	Weekly
Identify income tax–related items	Weekly
File necessary documents	Monthly
Monitor variances from spending plan	Weekly and monthly
Reconcile bank accounts	Monthly
Monitor net worth	Quarterly or yearly
Analyze interest rates on debt	Quarterly
Search for higher interest income on banking accounts	Quarterly
Check your credit report	Every four months
File an income tax return	Yearly
Evaluate your retirement plan and update beneficiaries	Yearly
Evaluate your investment allocations	Yearly
Evaluate your insurance needs	Yearly

Your goal should be to get these tasks done as efficiently and accurately as possible on a regular schedule. (They're all addressed in this book.) If it takes too long or is too complicated, you'll find other ways to spend your time. Especially if you don't like money management, you'll benefit from making it as easy and painless as possible. I recommend that you make a standing appointment with yourself each week for a couple hours to accomplish your money management tasks.

COMPUTER MONEY MANAGEMENT

I always suggest that you use the most advanced money management technology that's available. Once you get in a groove with online banking, online bill pay, and personal finance software or online applications, you'll find that they're incredibly easy and convenient to use. They'll streamline your efforts so you can get more done in less time. Programs can't do everything for you, but here are some of the benefits of using good financial software:

- See a one-page summary of your finances
- Create customized financial reports and graphs
- Gather all your bank and credit card accounts together in one place
- Import all your account data so you don't have to enter it manually
- Set up spending goals based on historical spending
- Track your budget process to see where you're overspending
- Prepare information for your tax return
- Categorize your expenses automatically
- Get automatic bill reminders so you never have late fees
- View upcoming bills so you can plan for them and avoid overdraft fees
- Build a plan to save for retirement or large purchases
- Stay aware of changes in your assets, liabilities, and net worth
- Create a plan to reduce debt

Here are some desktop software programs to consider using for your personal money management:

- **Quicken** at quicken.com is the best-known financial program with a variety of versions such as Starter, Deluxe, Mac, Home & Business, and Rental Property Manager, which range in price from approximately $30 to $150. You can manage multiple bank and credit accounts; manage your budget, bills, and loans; create reports and graphs; create tax documents; import online banking transactions; and more.

- **Moneydance.com** is a fully functional program that allows you to manage multiple bank and credit accounts; create and manage your budget, bills, and investments; use different currencies; create reports and graphs; import online banking transactions; and more. It supports Windows, Mac, and Linux, Solaris, OS/2, and Unix operating systems. The price is $39.99 and you can download a free demo version to try out.

- **iBank** at iggsoftware.com is a personal and small business financial manager for Mac users. It allows you to manage multiple bank and credit accounts; create and manage your budget, bills, loans, and investments; import online banking transactions; and more. The price is $59.99 and comes with a thirty-day guarantee.

- **Youneedabudget.com** (YNAB) is a budget manager that helps you prioritize spending by category; monitor spending trends; plan for future purchases; track multiple account balances; import online banking transactions; and more. The price is $59.95 and you can download a free seven-day demo version to try.

- **AceMoney** at mechcad.net is a free and fully functional program that allows you to manage multiple bank and credit accounts; create and manage your budget, bills, and investments; use different currencies; import online banking transactions; and more. It supports Windows, Mac, and Linux operating systems.

- **GnuCash** at gnucash.org is a free personal and small business financial manager for Windows, Mac, Linux, and Solaris users. It allows you to manage multiple bank accounts, enter your income and expenses by category, import online banking transactions, create reports, track investments, and more.

WHAT IS CLOUD COMPUTING?

Cloud computing allows you to accomplish tasks using free or low-cost services over the Internet instead of relying on software installed locally on your computer. The term *cloud* is used as a metaphor for the Internet's complex and abstract infrastructure. Google Docs at docs.google.com is a great example of a free cloud-based application. Users can create and share different kinds of documents that can be accessed from any computer with an Internet connection.

ONLINE FINANCIAL TOOLS

Many financial tools are now available as Web-based applications (instead of desktop-installed software) that allow you to work in the cloud. One of the best features of online applications and most online banking is a technology called "account aggregation," which allows networking to occur between all your financial institutions that offer online accounts. Services that utilize account aggregation securely compile data from all your financial accounts into a single Web site. That Web site could be your bank's online payment center or another online service, such as the ones I list below.

Aggregation is a great way to get an up-to-date and holistic view of your entire financial situation in one place. Checking multiple Web sites for account balances can be a real hassle. Go here and log in for your credit card transactions; go there and log in for your IRA balance. It's better to view all your financial accounts in one place with real-time balances. I used to waste a huge amount of time going to different Web sites to view updated information for my personal and business loans, credit cards, bank balances, and investment account balances. Now I just log in one place and see everything I need to know. Account aggregation saves you the trouble of having to remember multiple user names and passwords, too. It centralizes all your account data into one place. Here are some online financial aggregation tools to try that you can use from any Internet connection or from your mobile phone, in some cases:

- **Mint** at mint.com is a free money management application that aggregates your data, tracks your spending, monitors your budget and savings goals, and more. You can access all your balances and transactions together on the web or your iPhone. Mint makes personalized recommendations about how to save money.

- **Mvelopes** at mvelopes.com is a money management application with an emphasis on budgeting and monitoring your net worth. It aggregates data from thousands of financial institutions. You can get a fourteen-day free trial, then sign up for a plan that ranges from approximately $8 to $13 per month. Membership includes a full-featured online bill payment service for up to fifteen payments a month.

- **Myspendingplan.com** is a free online budgeting application that helps you create a budget, track your spending and savings goals, find coupons, set task alerts, and more.

- **Rudder** at rudder.com is a free money management application that aggregates your data, tracks your spending, budget goals, bill due dates, and monitors your cash flow.

- **Banks** such as Bank of America, RBC Bank, HSBC, and many others, have account aggregation integrated into their free online banking so you can track all of your financial accounts (not just the ones with those institutions). However, they may not offer the nifty functions and features of other online personal finance tools.

 Here's a quick and dirty tip: Make your online life easier and safer with a free version of the award-winning RoboForm automated password manager. Download it at roboform.com.

Don't Separate, Aggregate

Financial aggregation tools import, organize, and analyze your transaction data and account balances. Once your financial transactions get pulled in for the first time, you "tag" them to be identified with a particular spending or income category that you create. They monitor your spending, track budgets, and even create personalized recommendations. Even the applications that aren't banks use bank-level data security and don't require you to reveal account numbers, your Social Security number, or even your name.

To use account aggregation, you must first have online access and a log-on user name and password for each of the accounts that you want to pull into the aggregator. Here are the instructions that I followed for setting up my aggregator:

1. choose "View accounts from other Financial Institutions" from the main menu;
2. select "Add and manage accounts from Other Financial Institutions";
3. read the aggregation disclosures;
4. select the account type you wish to add (Banking, Credit Card, or Investment);
5. search for the bank or financial institution you wish to add.

It's that easy. As you add each financial institution, you provide the username and password you created to register at their Web site. You only have to do that one time; going forward, each account allows the aggregator to log in and export your data automatically.

I recommend using your bank's Web site for as many of the online functions that it offers, because they're usually free. When I log on to do online banking, my accounts are immediately aggregated to display their real-time balances. The aggregator fetches data from each of my online accounts to display fresh financial information. Not only can I see the accounts I have at that bank, such as my checking and money market deposit account, but the aggregator pulls in balances for each investment, loan, credit card, brokerage account, and bank account that I have at other institutions. I can track an unlimited number of accounts from each institution that's networked with my bank's aggregator. My bank can retrieve online data from thousands of institutions, with more being added to the network all the time. I enjoying viewing the aggregator and paying bills on the same Web site, but my bank doesn't offer some of the nice budgeting and savings features that you'll find on services like Mint.com.

Since most of the online financial services with aggregation are free or offer free trials, you can sign up and experiment with them at no risk. You'll need to see if your financial institutions, especially for your checking account and credit cards, are linked to these applications—otherwise they won't work. If your personal finances are relatively simple, you may find that free services offer enough functionality to properly manage your money. But if you use a variety of financial institutions, have many different types of accounts, or have a fairly complex tax situation, you'll benefit from using a comprehensive desktop program such as Quicken. That's because most financial software is fully customizable and gives you a variety of reports, budgeting, and tax functions that you won't find yet on online applications.

MONEY GIRL'S SYSTEM (THAT'S ME)

I'm going to share my personal money management system with you—but that doesn't necessarily mean it's right for you. The important point is that the job of good money management gets done. If you've been successful using a different method, good for you! But be honest with yourself about whether your system (or lack of one) is truly working to your advantage. If it isn't working, or you're open-minded about learning and using new technologies, branch out and try something new. If you don't like it or find that a new system isn't helpful, you can always go back to your old ways.

Paying Bills

For me, paying bills on time is a critical money management task. That's because late payments result in fees, financing charges, a reduced credit score, and less favorable status with many companies. Whether your income is a steady amount or fluctuates from week to week, you must practice the art of effective cash flow management. That means juggling your income and expenses so you're never spending more than what's in your checking account. If you've ever incurred hefty bank fees for having nonsufficient funds (NSF), you know how maddening that can be!

As I've mentioned, I use my bank's free online bill pay service, and I love it! I don't write or print checks except in very rare instances. I centralize all my bills on my bank's Web site.

Even though I could pay the power bill, insurance premiums, or home mortgage on those companies' separate Web sites, I prefer to pay all my bills in one place. That allows me to monitor what's coming due, what's in process, and what's already been paid, at a glance. Once you log in to a bill pay center, it's very easy to add a new bill. You simply enter the name of the person or company you want to pay, their address for remitting payment, and your customer account number (if applicable). The service either submits your payment electronically or mails out a paper check. You can create nicknames for each bill so they're easy to identify, such as "Laura's Car Insurance."

I choose to receive and pay as many bills electronically as possible. That reduces the amount of paper I have to handle and is

Here's a quick and dirty tip: Never go without overdraft protection on your checking account. At most banks, if you have a second account, such as a savings account or a line of credit, it can be linked to your checking (free of charge) in the event your checking account is temporarily overdrawn.

more earth-friendly. E-bills can be sent to your e-mail address, to your online bill pay center, or to both. You can set up any bill to be paid automatically on a certain date and to notify you when the payment is pending or completed. Another benefit of paying bills online is getting alerts. You can enter the typical due date for a bill and have an e-mail sent to you as a reminder that a bill's due soon or to notify you if it hasn't been paid by the due date you specify.

Some bills—such as for certain insurance premiums and loan payments that offer automatic withdrawals—I have set up to pay automatically because they're the same amount every month. For other bills that vary from month to month or don't offer automatic withdrawals, like my utilities or pest control service, I enter those manually. Once I receive a bill by e-mail, regular snail mail, or in my bank's online bill pay center, I set it up for payment right away. I don't wait to enter it for payment because the payment date can be set for up to a year into the future, and can be changed at any time. I log on to my bank's online bill pay center, enter the amount I want to pay, and the future date I want the company or person to receive my funds. If I've never paid them before, I have to add them as a payee first. After I save the payment, if I decide I want to change the payment date or to cancel it, I can do that at any time before the payment process begins. I recommend you designate one day a week as your official Personal Finance Day and update your bill pay center with all newly received bills. That ensures nothing falls through the cracks, and all your bills get paid on time!

 Here's a quick and dirty tip: Consider creating an e-mail account that's just for your finances, e-bills, and e-statements. Google's Gmail at mail.google.com is free and accessible from any computer or mobile phone with Internet access.

Categorizing Bills

After I set up a bill to pay online, the next step in my money management system is to enter it and categorize it in my financial software. Categorizing every transaction is the only way to analyze how you spend money and see if you're on target to meet an established spending plan. Detailed tracking of income and expenses also simplifies income tax filing at the end of the year. After I've entered all new bills into my online bill pay center, I manually enter them into my software check register. I've been a fan of QuickBooks desktop software for a long time because it allows me to manage both personal and business finances and is completely integrated with my online banking.

I enter each online bill payment in the register showing the future payment date and proper account classification. If it's a power bill that's due on the thirtieth of June, for example, the entry is dated June 30, with my chosen account as "utilities," and the payment amount. Doing a manual entry might seem like an unnecessary step, but it's important to my system because that's how I know if I have enough money in my account to cover upcoming bills and payments. At a glance I can see how much of my income is already spent and how much is committed to future expenses. That prevents me from spending money on anything else and also allows me to manage the excess. I can transfer leftover amounts in my checking account to a higher-interest account or send it as an extra payment on a loan, for example.

If you use an application like Mint.com, you can also create account types and enter your future bill payments there. It doesn't subtract future payments from your account balance the way desktop software does, but it ensures that you won't forget to account for a promised bill payment.

Most online banking services and credit card companies are integrated with Quicken and QuickBooks. If you use these programs as desktop software, you can easily download current bank account and credit card transactions directly into them at any time. That saves you the time and hassle of having to manually enter all your transactions. If you use an online application with account aggregation, your bank and credit card transactions get updated automatically each time you log in. On my Personal Finance Day, at the click of a button, I download all the transactions that have cleared my bank accounts into my QuickBooks software. Then I do the same for my credit card transactions that have posted. That pulls in all new transactions since my last download into my digital check register. The beauty of the software is that it recognizes what's already there and never duplicates income or expense transactions in a register. So when the power bill that I entered in my QuickBooks register a month ago is now paid and appears as a deduction in my bank checking account, the software automatically "matches" it to the download. That insures that only new and unique transactions get pulled into the register. Any "unmatched" transaction must be assigned a specific payee or payer name and an account, which is quick and easy to do. The software will remember that certain payees should get a specific account classification. For example, charges made to Skip's Supermarket will always be assigned a "grocery" classification after you do it manually the first time. But if you buy a prescription from the pharmacy at Skip's Supermarket and want to classify it as "medical," it's easy to make that change.

For software users, you should have a separate register for each account. For example, you can set one up for checking, savings, loans, credit cards, and so on. Credit card transactions should be downloaded to their own register, not to your checking account register. Doing that would result in a duplication of transactions once you pay the monthly credit card bill from your checking account. Credit card accounts should ideally be zero-balance accounts because at the end of a period, the charges should be offset by your full payment to the credit card company. You need the detail in the credit card register to accurately categorize each charge you make.

Keeping Track of Your Tax Items

Having a good system for identifying tax-related items is something you will thank yourself for each year at tax time. We'll cover what you need to know about taxes in chapter 10. But here are some items that you might need to keep track of throughout the year for tax purposes:

- Medical expenses
- Dental expenses
- Education expenses
- Real estate taxes
- Investment interest
- Business expenses if you're self-employed
- Job-seeking expenses
- Gifts to charity
- Property losses due to theft or unexpected events
- Gambling losses
- Unreimbursed employee expenses
- Tax preparation fees

Doing your own taxes or even just preparing your information for a tax professional can be one of life's miseries. I dread it. So I do everything possible during the year to make filing tax returns as simple and easy as possible. This is where accounting software really shines. Whether you bank online or not, if you classify income and expenses accurately throughout the year in a financial program, getting ready for taxes should be pretty effortless. Since you can create as many unique account classifications as you like, you can be precise about how you want to identify specific expenses.

Let's say you go to the grocery store and buy food for yourself plus office supplies for your part-time home business. It may seem easy to circle the office supplies as a business expense and throw the receipt into a file with others to add up at tax time. But breaking up the expenses and categorizing each of them, sooner rather than later, will save time and effort down the road. Whether you enter the transaction manually or download it into your software from your online bank or credit card account, it's painless to split out the purchase into the correct amounts for accounts titled "Groceries" and "Internet business," for example. I would still make a notation on the receipt about the reason for the business expense and file it, in the event of a tax audit. If you use the services of an accountant, you can send her a copy of your electronic files in addition to the year-end documents you receive. Most accountants are very comfortable with Quicken and QuickBooks. The best accountants will request that you complete an annual tax questionnaire, analyze your software data and submitted documents, and perhaps ask some necessary follow-up questions.

Computerizing Your Budget

Another benefit of having income and expenses properly classified by account is that it makes it simple to monitor variances from your spending plan. Most personal finance and business accounting software allow you to set up budgets and track them against your actual income and expenses. After you have a year of data, the next year's spending plan can be based on the numbers from the prior year or altered as you like. Budgeting tools are very useful if you can account for all purchases, including those made with cash. A good way to handle cash purchases is to first record the source of the cash. For example, if you withdraw $50 from an ATM, record it as a "cash withdrawal expense." Be diligent about keeping each receipt for your cash purchases. Perhaps you spend the cash this way: $40 on a restaurant dinner, $5 on a couple cups of coffee, and $5 on a magazine. If you have the receipts from each of your cash purchases, you can correctly reclassify the $50 from "cash withdrawal expense" to $45 for "dining" and $5 for "magazines," for instance. I don't make many cash purchases, but when I do, that's how I account for every penny of it.

Spending with Plastic

For purchases that I make to my rewards credit card (more on rewards credit cards in the next chapter), I download them into my financial software once a week, just like I do with transactions in my bank accounts. Here's how: I log on to my online credit card account, click the "download to software" button, and import transactions into the credit card register in QuickBooks. I make it a habit to send an extra payment to the credit card company each month. Every other week I see what my rewards card balance is, and set up that amount to pay. Could I wait and pay the entire credit card balance off on the last possible day of the billing period? Yes. But I have an aversion to using credit cards in the first place, so paying the bill more frequently improves my mind-set about it. I get the rewards and savings from the credit card, while basically accounting for the purchases as deductions from my checking balance right away, just like using a debit card. When I receive bills from companies that accept my rewards credit card, I pay with it, instead of initiating an electronic transfer or a check through my online bill pay center. That allows me to keep piling on the cash rewards. I'll talk more about how to use rewards credit cards to your advantage in the next chapter.

Reconciling Bank Accounts

Reconciling bank accounts is another important task in my money management system. Reconciliation is the process of confirming that the balance you think you have matches the amount that the bank shows you have. It's best to reconcile each account as soon as you receive the monthly statement. The first part of a statement lists the beginning balance, the total amount of deposits, the total amount of withdrawals, and the ending balance for a given period of time. The beginning balance for one period should be the same as the ending balance for the prior period. The next part of a statement shows detail about deposits, credits, checks, and withdrawals.

Reconciling accounts in accounting software is a simple process. If you bank online and are in the habit of downloading new transactions into your software on a regular basis, it's even easier because there are rarely any surprise transactions. If you follow my system, you'll be able to match your current online balances to your various account and credit card registers by date.

If you don't utilize online banking, but instead enter transactions manually into a paper register, reconciling your account on a monthly basis is critical. It's very important because the reconciliation process is the best way to discover:

- Fraudulent use of your account
- Fraudulent use of your debit card
- Unexpected bank fees
- A forgotten purchase

It's always easier to resolve problems or disputes with the bank sooner rather than later. Once you find a discrepancy, you can make a correcting entry in your register. If you don't reconcile accounts on a regular basis, you may mistakenly believe that you have more money in the account than you really do. If this were the case, you might spend more than you have, and potentially rack up lots of nonsufficient funds fees. Ouch!!!

But if you adapt to online banking and download your transactions on a regular basis, entering each debit card receipt becomes a chore of the past. However, you'll still need to enter receipts for cash purchases—there's no way to avoid entering those manually. It's a good idea to keep all your receipts so you can verify the accuracy of the amount that clears your account. Then you can shred the receipts and throw them away. However, if you make purchases related to your job or business, it's a good idea to note on the receipt why the purchase was made and to file it. That way if you're ever audited by the IRS, you'll have documentation about why a particular expense was tax-deductible—and you won't need to rely on your memory.

SAMPLE BANKING SETUPS

Now that we've covered banking accounts and money management systems, take a look at the sample banking setup diagrams that I've included. They should help you visualize different ways you can configure your own system. The goal is to make receiving, spending, and tracking the flow of your money as simple and profitable as possible.

SAMPLE BANKING SETUP DIAGRAM #1

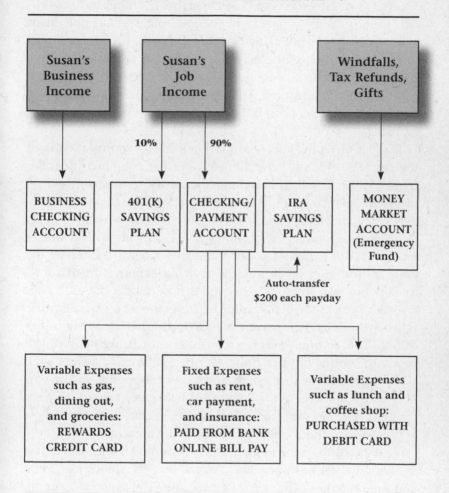

Diagram #1 is a banking setup for Susan. She needs to capture income from three sources: a part-time dog-walking business, a full-time computer programming job, and additional income such as refunds or gifts received. The payments from her business clients usually come as checks in the mail but she has one client who prefers to pay her using PayPal. Her PayPal account is linked to her business checking account at Bank of the Best, so these funds get electronically deposited there. She likes Bank of the Best because it's FDIC-insured and has a convenient local branch, which she uses to deposit her dog-walking checks every Saturday morning.

For her other income, Susan has personal accounts at Bank of the Best. She elects to have 10 percent of her computer programming paycheck sent to her company's 401(k) retirement savings plan. The balance of her after-tax paycheck is electronically deposited to her checking account every other Friday. Whenever Susan receives a cash gift or a refund of any kind, she saves it in her money market deposit account that earns 1 percent interest. She keeps a minimum of six months of living expenses in that low-interest, but safe, account. Her goal is to max out her IRA each year. Through Bank of the Best's online banking, she set up an automatic transfer to occur each payday for $200 from her checking to her Schwab IRA account. Susan pays all her bills using Bank of the Best's free online bill pay center. For her daily expenditures such as buying gas for her car, lunch, and grocery shopping, she uses an American Express rewards credit card that gives her a cash back credit. Where her card isn't accepted she uses her Bank of the Best Visa debit card that's linked to her checking account.

Every Saturday morning is Susan's Personal Finance Day. After she deposits her business checks at the branch, she comes home and logs on to her Bank of the Best account. The aggregator on the home page instantly fetches data from all three of her deposit accounts, both of her retirement accounts, and her credit card account, so she can see their current balances at a glance. Susan clicks on her checking account, clicks on the "download to software" button and exports all deposit, withdrawal, and debit card transactions that have cleared her checking account since the last time she exported data last Saturday. She opens her financial software, Quicken, which has her newly imported checking transactions waiting for her to manage with just a couple clicks. Susan categorizes each transaction by assigning it an account, such as dining out, utilities, or rent, for example. Most of the payees already have a corresponding account memorized, so it's just a matter of clicking a button to approve it. For example, her software has memorized that purchases made at Polly's Paninis are "dining out," so each one automatically gets categorized as such, unless Susan decides to change it. Susan also downloads transactions for her money market and business checking account the same way. Her software knows that data from those accounts go to their dedicated registers.

Every month Susan receives a statement from Bank of the Best for her three bank accounts. Her software has a reconciliation function that she uses to match up transactions on each statement to those in each register. That way she's confident that everything is accounted for and she didn't miss any unexpected bank fees or errors.

Next, Susan logs on to her American Express online account and clicks on "recent activity," then on the "download" button. Again, each charge and payment gets automatically entered into Susan's credit card register in her software after she categorizes it and accepts it. That creates a negative balance in the credit card register because those transactions represent money that Susan owes to American Express. Each time she pays the credit card bill in full, her checking register is reduced and her credit card register is increased back to zero.

The second banking setup diagram is for a couple named Donna and Richard. Donna's in sales and Richard is an engineer. Since Donna's paychecks vary from month to month and Richard's do not, they decided to deposit their income in separate accounts. Donna's paycheck is electronically deposited into two FDIC-insured online accounts with HSBC Direct: 90 percent goes to their payment account (earning 0.85 percent) and 10 percent to their savings account (earning 1.35 percent). The online savings account is where they keep emergency funds equal to one year's worth of living

SAMPLE BANKING SETUP DIAGRAM #2

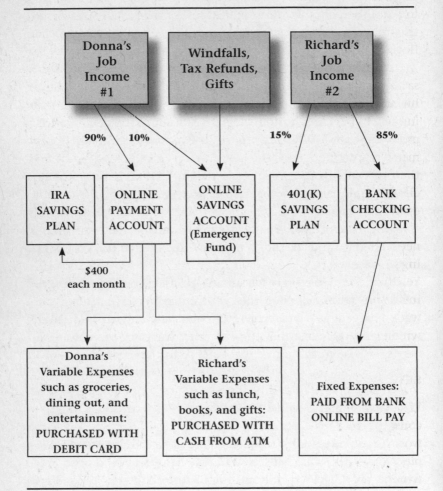

expenses. Donna's income is used for the couple's everyday spending such as groceries, dining out, and entertainment. She likes the convenience of using a debit card, but Richard prefers to spend cash that he withdraws for free from a local ATM. Donna's goal is to max out her IRA (we'll get to IRAs in chapter 7), so she logs on to the online payment account and transfers $400 into her E*Trade IRA account each month.

Richard invests 15 percent of his income in his workplace 401(k) savings plan (we'll get to 401(k)s in chapter 7, too). The balance of his net paycheck is electronically deposited into a local bank checking account. He logs on to the bank's online bill pay center twice a month to enter any paper bills he received and to initiate all payments that are due. Then he imports transactions that have cleared their three accounts into iBank software. He uses iBank to reconcile those three bank accounts each month when he receives the e-statements.

What does your banking diagram look like? Consider if you need to add a different type of account, such as a high-yield checking, or if you should set up automatic transfers between accounts. Your goal should be to have accounts that earn the highest rates of interest and are integrated with your financial programs and software. That way, your money management tasks can be accomplished with as much accuracy and convenience as possible.

SETTING YOUR ROUTINE

When you create a schedule to accomplish your financial tasks, consider "batching" the work. Batching means that you do more work less often rather than doing less work more often. For example, instead of paying bills on a daily basis, you would do it on a weekly or biweekly schedule. The idea behind batching is that starting and stopping any task invites inefficiency. On the other hand, once you begin a task and get focused on what you're doing, you have the potential to accomplish more in less time. I recommend that you pay bills, categorize transactions, and monitor spending plans on a weekly basis. Account reconciliations should be completed as soon as you receive an account statement each month.

Prompt reconciliations will alert you to any discrepancies that need to be addressed and make certain that you know the exact balance in your account.

The end of each quarter (March 31, June 30, September 30, and December 31) is a good time to update your Personal Financial Statement. That task forces you to recalculate your net worth and to consider other factors important to good money management. I reviewed bank accounts in chapter 3. I recommend that for each deposit account you have, list the rate of interest you earn on your PFS. Your goal is to get the highest return for your dollars, while still keeping them safe. Each quarter, do some research to see if there are better options to earn more interest on your deposit accounts. A couple more quarterly and yearly tasks are to analyze (1) the interest rate you're paying on debt and (2) your investment allocations. I'll cover more about both in upcoming chapters.

STAYING SAFE FROM IDENTITY THEFT

One of the reasons you should reconcile your accounts each month is to stay safe from becoming a victim of identity theft. Identity theft is the fastest-growing crime in the United States. It happens when someone steals your personal information and uses it to commit fraud or other types of crime without your knowledge. A thief could use your name, Social Security number, driver's license number, or various bank or credit card numbers, for instance, to wreak havoc in your life.

Once your identity is jeopardized, getting it cleared up can cost time and money, not to mention leaving you with a really botched credit report. That could be a real detriment to your financial health. After a thief gets your personal information they can attempt to open new checking or credit card accounts in your name, spend like there's no tomorrow, and leave you with the unpaid bills. Thieves have been known to take out auto loans and even file tax returns in the name of their victims.

Take every precaution to guard yourself against this terrible crime. Thieves can steal your wallet or copy your credit or debit card numbers. But they can also steal your mail or "dumpster dive" for

Here's a quick and dirty tip: If you make purchases with paper checks, carry as few with you as possible. If a thief steals a pad of checks from you, they can do a tremendous amount of damage to your finances in a short period of time.

information in your trash or at businesses. Sometimes, criminals actually change your mailing address so that your mail gets sent to them, giving them access to your confidential information and account numbers. If you become a victim of identity theft, go to idtheft.gov to report it and to learn about your rights.

7 Tips to Prevent Identity Theft

Here are seven tips to help you protect yourself against identity fraud:

1. Guard your Social Security card and number like a junkyard dog! Remove the card from your wallet—leave it in a safe place at home or in a safe-deposit box. If you have other cards that include the number, but you want to carry them all the time (such as for health insurance), consider carrying a copy of the card, with the number blacked-out, instead of carrying the actual card.

2. Never print your Social Security number on your checks or share it with any person or company that you don't trust 100 percent. There are only a handful of situations where you might need to reveal the number, such as for new employment, opening accounts with financial institutions, tax-related matters, or applying for credit or insurance policies.

3. When shopping or submitting personal information online, make sure the Web site is encrypted. A secure Web address will begin with "https" instead of "http." Also look for a closed padlock symbol at the bottom or top of the Web page that indicates a secure

connection. Click on the padlock icon to determine if the security certificate is up-to-date.

4. Never use your Social Security number, or any part of it, as your user name or password for online accounts. If a password was automatically issued to you using those numbers, be sure to promptly change it.

5. Never carry any financial cards, checks, or ID that you don't need to.

6. Shred all documents that have any personal information or account numbers on them, including unwanted credit card offers.

7. Follow up on missing statements or bills. If they haven't arrived in the mail, it could indicate that someone has changed your mailing address. Consider going paperless with e-statements and e-bills when possible.

What About Credit Monitoring?

A service that's becoming more popular is credit monitoring. For a monthly fee, services such as LifeLock (lifelock.com) and Identity Guard (identityguard.com) watch for changes to your credit report for you. They may also provide identity theft insurance, computer security software, and wireless Internet protection, for example. They claim to monitor black market Web sites for account numbers that match yours. Those cyberhangouts are where criminals gather to sell and exchange stolen information, such as credit card numbers. The cost for these services may be justified if the identity theft crime rate continues to skyrocket or if you've already been a victim of identity fraud. With good information and some common sense, you can do a good job of protecting yourself. No one can be 100 percent protected from identity theft, but you can do everything in your power to become a more difficult target.

5

Dealing with Debt

Procrastination is like a credit card: It's a lot of fun until you get the bill.
—CHRISTOPHER PARKER, actor

There's good news and bad news when it comes to debt. The good news is that household debt in the United States has decreased slightly recently according to data at federalreserve.gov. That's a sign that many people are borrowing less and paying down their credit card balances. The bad news, however, is that we still have too much debt relative to our income. When you can't seem to make room in your spending plan for savings and investments to meet your financial goals, it's likely that you've financed more than you can really afford. In this chapter, I'll show you some smart strategies and moves to lower your monthly debt obligations so you can free up extra cash.

If you think that I've never struggled with having too much debt or worried about how to pay off a growing credit card balance, I can tell you that you're dead wrong. In the introduction to this book, I mentioned that after I graduated from college and started working, I racked up some serious credit card debt that I carried right into my marriage. No one is immune from making financial mistakes, having poor judgment from time to time, or simply procrastinating doing what they know they need to do. The fact that you're reading this book means you're ready to take responsibility for your financial health. I know that once you get into financial debt, it's often easier to fall further behind than to dig yourself out. I don't want you to dwell on past mistakes and beat yourself up about them, because that never helps. No matter what your situation, or how or why you got into debt in the first place, you can get out of debt. Keep reading and I'll show you exactly how to do it.

DO YOU NEED TO ELIMINATE ALL DEBT?

But first, I want to make some general comments about debt because there seems to be a growing movement in the United States toward reducing and eliminating it altogether and that's not necessarily the smartest thing to do. There are good debts and bad debts. Debt that allows you to make money is good; debt that causes you to lose money is bad. For example, an affordable home mortgage is generally a good debt because it allows you to buy a home that can appreciate in value over time. An auto loan is generally a bad debt (even though it may be a necessary one for most people) because vehicles depreciate quickly and rarely make money for the owner. You get the idea—going into debt for vacations, clothes, electronics, or furniture, for example, is not a wise investment in your future.

Believe me, I'm a strong proponent of keeping debt as low as possible. But the issue isn't whether a mortgage or business loan is inherently a bad thing, because it isn't. The issue is whether you use a mortgage or a business loan to buy something that you can't afford in the first place. Buying a home that's way out of your price range is never wise, no matter how low the payments on an adjustable-rate mortgage might be in the early years, for example.

The amount of debt that's acceptable for anyone is a highly personal evaluation. There are many factors to consider, such as future income, comfort level with risk, and net worth, for example. If you have debt, but also have plenty of income to cover it in addition to a sufficient emergency reserve fund, you probably don't have a financial dilemma. But if you use debt to consistently finance a lifestyle that you can't afford, or are paying sky-high interest rates, it

Here's a quick and dirty tip: Calculate your debt-to-income ratio to see if your debt is too high for the amount of money you make. Add up all your monthly debt payments and divide that number by your monthly pretax income. Ideally, that ratio should not be more than 36 percent.

should be addressed sooner rather than later. If you have debt that's grown out of control or that weighs you down psychologically, now's the time to take swift action to repair the trouble. Many times there's a snowball effect that happens with debt—one bad decision after another causes it to accumulate rapidly. Once that happens, many people give up because they simply don't know how to get their debt under control. And even if you're not drowning under unmanageable debt, it's wise to understand what your debt really costs you.

MAKE A DEBT REDUCTION PLAN

The first step in getting a handle on your debt is to assess your overall financial situation. This is where the Personal Financial Statement (PFS) that you created in chapter 2 comes into play again. So if you haven't created it yet, take some time to gather up your information. You should have a column that lists the interest rate for each of your debts. If you have debts with variable interest rates, you'll need to update your PFS with current information and reevaluate it on a regular basis, like once a quarter. You should also have a second column for the maturity or pay-off date on each of your installment loans. For your credit lines or credit cards you can enter an "X" since there is no specified maturity date for those types of debt. Now, I'd like you to add a third a column and title it "pay-off priority." The interest rate, maturity date, and pay-off priority data will help you compare each of your debts objectively, based on the numbers.

In addition to good debt and bad debt, there's also short-term and long-term debt. Short-term debts are those with a maturity date less than five to ten years in the future (or none at all, as with credit cards). Short-term debts are the most dangerous ones—the ones I'll urge you to pay off first. They have the greatest potential and likelihood of really getting you into further trouble. They can turn a slight problem into a bad one, and a bad problem into something absolutely devastating! In other words, time is of the essence for certain debts. Long-term debts have a maturity date of ten years or more from the date you took out the loan. Long-term debt is generally considered good debt. You shouldn't have excessive long-term debt for your level of income, but it has some redeeming qualities that make it not quite so dangerous. Your long-term debt might include installment loans secured by assets, such as mortgages; debts that come with an allowable tax deduction, such as mortgages, HE-LOCs, and student loans; and debt that could potentially raise your net worth, such as a business loan. Paying off long-term debts will fall lower on the priority scale.

Take a look at all of your liabilities on your PFS, and rank your top priority short-term debt as enemy number one. A debt that's owed to the IRS or due to litigation is very serious and must be wiped out first, because the government has more power over your life than anyone else you may owe. Therefore, they can cause you the most misery if you don't settle your debts with them! The next in line for elimination should be any loan or bill that's already in default, or in the hands of a collections agency, such as an unpaid medical bill, because delinquencies usually result in hefty late fees as well as bad marks on your credit report. Your next highest priority debts should be payroll loans, vehicle loans, or credit accounts that charge the highest rates of interest. For example, a vehicle loan with 12 percent interest should be a higher priority than a credit card balance with a 10 percent interest rate. A small balance on a department store credit card that charges 18 percent interest should be paid off before a larger balance on a credit card with 14 percent interest, because on a percentage basis, higher-interest debt costs you more, and therefore should be ranked as a higher priority for elimination.

I want to make the point that in some cases short-term debt is not the result of unnecessary spending. Unpaid medical bills can pile up if you have to go without health insurance or get caught sick between jobs. Loans taken to purchase vehicles are one of the most important but worst investments most of us are forced to make for the sake of transportation. I'm a realist. I recognize that having short-term debt can be something you don't choose to have. In some cases it's a lifeline to help you survive a real emergency such as the temporary loss of a job or business. Nevertheless, it's important to work hard at getting rid of the most toxic liabilities you have, so they don't eat up your paycheck.

After you've prioritized your short-term debts, do the same for your remaining long-term liabilities. If you have a mortgage and are like most people, it's likely that you won't pay it off until you reach old-age or perhaps stumble on a winning lottery ticket! So, it's smart to reduce the amount of interest you'll pay over the life of your long-term loans. You can save money by doing a loan refinance, modification, or consolidation. Keep reading to find out more about those great options to reduce your debts. Again, use the interest rates on your long-term debts as the primary indicator for their payoff priority. Rank a home loan with a 10 percent fixed or variable interest rate as a higher priority than a 5 percent student loan, for example. Whether you'll take an allowable tax deduction on a loan is an important consideration because the tax savings will reduce the after-tax interest rate you pay. A lower interest rate makes the debt less expensive and therefore more tolerable. As I mentioned, mortgages, HELOCs, and student loans all come with tax deductions for taxpayers who are eligible.

Use Assets to Pay Down Debts

After you've analyzed your debts and ranked their payoff priority, reexamine assets on your Personal Financial Statement. Many people like their assets so much that they're willing to keep them despite being over their heads in debt. I understand that reducing a cash account or selling a financial investment to pay down your liabilities can be difficult. But you should always use your existing assets such as savings and investments outside of retirement accounts to pay down short-term debts when you can. Do you own anything that you could sell to raise cash? If so, paying off an 18 percent consumer debt on a credit card is just like finding an investment with an 18 percent rate of return that's tax free! However, I don't recommend selling or borrowing against retirement accounts to pay off debt, because the taxes and penalties for doing so are too high and I'll cover more about that in chapter 7. Nor do I recommend using every penny of your cash to eliminate debt. It's still important to leave yourself a cash cushion of an emergency fund that would keep you safe in a crisis situation, such as the loss of a job.

"Optimize" Your Debts

If you can't pay off a debt with existing assets, consider how your debts could be juggled to lower your interest rates and fees until you can pay it off. Shifting your debt from higher-interest accounts to lower-interest options is called optimizing your debt. Optimizing certainly doesn't make debt disappear, but it does reduce what you have to pay in interest. Do you have a low-interest HELOC that's large enough to accommodate balances you can transfer from higher-interest credit cards or loans? How about a friend or relative who's willing to offer you a low-interest loan that you pay back over a few months? See what resources you already have that you're not using to pay off your debts or to shift balances so that your debt will cost you less until you can eliminate it.

BALANCE TRANSFER CREDIT CARDS

A common way to optimize consumer debt is to use a balance transfer credit card. It's a special type of card that charges 0 percent or very low interest during a promotional period, which typically ranges from three months to a year. You can pay off higher-interest debt, such as a credit card or car loan, and save a substantial amount of interest. The amount you can transfer is subject to the credit limit you're offered. Additionally, there's usually a transfer fee in the range of 2 percent to 5 percent for each balance that you move to a transfer card.

Doing a balance transfer is a good strategy if, and only if, you know for sure that you can pay off the balance in full by the offer's expiration date. If not, the resulting interest rate is likely to be higher than what you're currently paying. Here's a situation where doing a balance transfer makes sense:

> Let's say you're having a good year at work and are going to receive a $5,000 bonus within six months. You plan to use the bonus to wipe out your $4,000 credit card debt. Instead of waiting for the bonus, you can pay off the balance with a new transfer card that charges 0 percent interest for six months with a 2 percent or $80 ($4,000×0.02) transfer fee. You won't be charged any minimum payments during the six-month promotional period. If your minimum payment on the old card was $120, now you can save that amount each month instead. Over six months you could save $640, which is $720 ($120×6) without the $80 transfer fee. Once you receive your bonus you would pay off the transfer card in full, before the 0 percent offer expires.

But if you're not positive that you can pay off your full balance in time, don't risk doing a balance transfer. When the music stops playing and the low rate ends, you might get stuck with a huge, double-digit interest rate on your debt, and few options to improve the situation. You could try to transfer the debt to another low-rate card right away, but if you're not approved for one, all the savings you had hoped to gain from doing a balance transfer would be lost. You'd probably be worse off than if you hadn't done a balance transfer in the first place. So always have a solid exit strategy for paying your balance off before the promotional rate on a balance transfer card disappears.

Before you pull the trigger on doing a transfer, make sure that you understand all the card terms. Be extremely cautious; there are severe penalties buried in the fine print that can sneak up on you. For example, one late payment on most balance transfer cards results in a rate hike into the stratosphere. Many default rates can go as high as 29.99 percent! Yikes!

Here's a quick and dirty tip: Use the Balance Transfer Calculator at creditcards.com to see how much you could save by doing a transfer. Then find up-to-date offers at sites like balancetransfers.com, cardratings.com, and creditcards.com.

Here are important features of transfer credit cards to evaluate:

1. The interest rate charged for transfers made during the promotional period
2. The interest rate charged after the promotional period. (That's only important, of course, if you don't pay off the card in full or if you plan to use the card afterward.)
3. The duration of the low-rate promotional offer
4. The balance transfer fees
5. The annual card fee

When choosing a transfer card, look for one with no annual fee, the lowest transfer fee, and the lowest promotional rate that lasts the longest period of time.

USE CREDIT CARDS WISELY

Since we're already on the subject of credit cards, now is the perfect time to talk about them more in depth—especially since they have become such an easy way for many people to get into debt. Because credit cards often lead to financial trouble, I've devoted a section of this chapter just to them. Purchases made on bank credit cards and retail store cards can derail even the best financial intentions. No one seems to be immune from the perils of plastic—not the young, old, educated, uneducated, wealthy, or poor. Even this author (who considers herself pretty astute when it comes to financial matters) has been led astray by the calls of shopping sirens and a shiny credit card in her wallet. It's an equal opportunity threat because credit cards remain relatively easy to obtain. Even those with poor credit can often get a high interest credit card—what a recipe for disaster! Does that mean credit cards are evil? Absolutely not. The truth is, it's just a piece of plastic that happens to be a powerful financial tool.

The problem with credit cards is that they can be accessories to a financially dishonest life—something you really can't afford. Most short-term debt finances a lifestyle, rather than the purchase of genuine assets that hold their value over time. Once charges are made to a credit card, for example, what do you have to show for them? You might have more clothes, furniture, gifts, electronics, or dinners out—which is all great stuff to buy if you can truly afford it. But it's likely that you spent money on something you really didn't need in the first place, and now that money is gone.

Many people think that it's okay to carry a credit card balance as long as they're making the minimum monthly payment. Please understand that just making the minimum payment isn't sufficient, because you're still accumulating interest on the balance you carry forward each month. If your minimum payment is less than the interest charged each month, your credit card balance can actually still grow! It's kind of like getting stuck in quicksand—each effort forward seems to pull you back down. So the trick to eliminating credit card debt is to stop charging and to make progressively larger payments at the same time. If you have credit card debt, make a commitment to yourself that you will not make another purchase on the card, whatever it takes.

One of the best ways to use a credit card as part of your money management system is to pretend that it's not really a credit card, but a debit card. That might sound like a silly mind game, but if it works, so what?

Credit Card Benefits

I want to point out that credit cards have a good side, too. They're a financial tool that many of us can benefit from in our money management strategy. Notice I said many of us, not all of us! For some, a credit card is a plastic invitation to reckless behavior. For others, responsible use brings nice rewards and benefits. If you approach credit cards with discipline and self-control, then you'll have a healthy lifelong relationship with them.

Consider these benefits that can come with responsible credit card use:

1. **Build or improve your credit rating.** Building up credit is very important for those just starting out. A good credit rating will open up a world of financial possibilities for you. You can build or improve your credit rating by paying credit card bills on time and never maxing out your available credit limit. If your credit rating is less than perfect, demonstrating responsible credit card use is one of the fastest ways to improve your credit score.

2. **Get payment float time.** The second major benefit of paying for purchases with a credit card is getting float time. That's the amount of time between receiving the goods or services you charge and actually having to pay for them. For example, if you pay for a new television with a debit card, the funds are taken out of your account within a day or two. But if you pay with a credit card, you have a free grace period of anywhere from twenty to thirty days to submit payment. That means your money stays in your control longer. If you charge $3,000 on average each month and earn 1 percent on the balance in your checking account, a float time of thirty days earns you an extra $360 in interest per year.

3. **Have the ability to dispute charges.** Credit cards are a preferred method of payment for large purchases. That's true not only because you can rack up some nice rewards, but because you have the ability to dispute charges. Any defective merchandise or service problem that isn't resolved to your satisfaction can be taken up with the card's issuer. They'll work on your behalf to settle the issue and can suspend or reverse the charge on your account. Certain cards also offer built-in insurance for products or travel-related services.

4. **Safe to use.** The fourth benefit of using credit cards is that they're relatively safe to use when compared to checks or cash. The law is on the consumer's side when it comes to lost or stolen credit cards. The Fair Credit Billing Act, established by the U.S. Federal Trade Commission, addresses these issues. It says that your maximum

liability for unauthorized use of a credit card is $50. And if you have the card in your possession, but someone stole your credit card number, your liability is $0. So there is no significant financial risk to making purchases with a credit card.

WHAT KIND OF CREDIT CARD SHOULD YOU USE?

Another benefit to using credit cards is the variety of credit cards offered. To determine the best one for you, it's helpful to narrow them down to four broad categories: student, rewards, low-interest, and secured.

1. **Student credit cards** are a great way for young people to begin building credit because they generally don't require an established credit rating for approval. However, for anyone under 21, card issuers require proof of income or that you have an approved adult co-signer on the account. Many student cards offer additional benefits such as cash back rewards. The downside to student cards is that they charge higher interest rates than other types of cards. A naïve and irresponsible student could cause a world of financial pain for themselves if they rack up debt that they can't pay off in full.

2. **Rewards credit cards** are ideal for the most responsible credit card users and offer users rewards for their purchases in different forms, like cash and airline tickets, for example. They work wonders if you charge a majority of your purchases on the card and then pay off the full balance each month. You can also charge selective purchases on the card based on how the reward system works. I've been doing it for years and it really helps me get the most out of my spending. I use the American Express Blue Cash rewards card right now that offers 5 percent cash back on gasoline, grocery, and pharmacy purchases and 1.25 percent cash back on everything else after you hit a $6,500 spending threshold.

Here's how a rewards card can work for you:

Let's say you have $3,000 a month in purchases and bills that you can pay for with a rewards credit card. If $1,000 worth of those purchases qualifies for the top-tier reward at 5 percent cash back, and the remaining $2,000 gets 1.25 percent cash back, that's $75 a month or $900 a year in total cash back. I'll take it!

Of course, if you don't pay off your balance in full each month, the interest you'll owe will more than offset your rewards. For example, a credit card with an annual percentage rate (APR) of 16.99 percent comes to 1.42 percent per month. If you were to carry over a $3,000 balance at that interest rate for just one month, it would cost you $42.60. Then if you were to do it again the next month, a $6,000 balance would be $85.20, and so forth.

If I had to carry a balance over from month to month, using the rewards card would not be the smartest card choice. That's because rewards credit cards generally don't offer the lowest interest rates.

I want to stress that using a rewards credit card for purchases, as I've described for my system, is an advanced technique. It's not for anyone who's demonstrated out-of-control spending patterns. If you (1) are a money management novice, (2) have had difficulty paying off credit card balances in the past, or (3) have unmanageable debt, I don't recommend tempting fate. If you have a problem managing your spending, and you carry around a credit card long enough, you're bound to make some flawed decisions.

3. **Low-interest credit cards** are great for doing balance transfers, which was covered earlier. That's a strategy to save money on interest by moving an existing balance to a low or zero-interest card before you pay it off in full. The lowest rates are usually just introductory offers that could last anywhere from three months to a year. You can get some substantial savings during that time. However, if you miss a payment during the offer period, the card usually reverts to a much higher rate. If you transfer a big balance but aren't able to pay it off within the offer period, a low-rate card may actually charge you higher interest than the card you started with!

4. **Secured credit cards** are for the least responsible card users because they require a prepaid balance as collateral. They may de-

mand payment of several hundred dollars as a deposit with your application. They also charge high interest rates and annual fees. However, if you got into trouble with credit cards in the past, paying for a secured credit card may be a good strategy to get on the road to credit recovery.

WHAT'S A VIRTUAL CREDIT CARD?

A virtual credit card gives you a unique, disposable number for each purchase, instead of using the real account number on a card. This gives you an extra layer of protection because the temporary number can be used just once, or in some cases again with the same merchant. You and your credit card company are the only ones who know your real credit card number. You can use it to make purchases online, over the phone, or by mail. However, you couldn't use a virtual credit card if you have to present a physical card to verify your purchase, such as for a rental car reservation or getting concert tickets at will-call, for example. Since the merchant only sees your virtual number, your real information can never be saved in their database. If a hacker gets into the merchant's database, the number they could steal would generally be useless to them.

A Word of Warning: Canceling Cards May Be Bad for Your Credit

Many people have gone wild with frugality, closed their credit card accounts, and grinned as they chopped up the cards. That's wonderful, but is it possible that canceling a credit card could hurt your credit score? The overwhelming answer is "yes." Anything that increases your credit utilization ratio lowers your credit score. Here's an example:

Let's say you have two credit cards and each one has a $1,000 limit. That gives you a total credit limit of $2,000. If you charge $500 to the first card and $0 to the second one, your total utilization ratio is 25 percent ($500÷$2,000=0.25 or 25 percent). If you decide to cancel the second card because you don't use it anymore, your utilization ratio doubles to 50 percent! The calculation is now $500÷$1,000=0.50 or 50 percent.

One strategy to avoid a ding to your credit is to request a credit limit increase on the first card from $1,000 to $2,000. If your average balance remains at $500, having a $2,000 limit would lower your credit utilization ratio back down to 25 percent for that card. That's low enough to cancel your second card without hurting your credit score.

Some card issuers have tightened up their credit rules and closed accounts for inactivity or slashed credit limits on accounts in good standing. They may view your unused cards with high credit limits as a potential risk. So, it may actually be beneficial to make small charges on cards that you rarely use and pay them off in full, in order to keep them active. Having a card canceled, or your credit limit lowered, leaves you with less available credit which can easily raise your credit utilization ratio and cause your credit score to drop.

Since your credit score is based on other factors (which I'll get to next), there are other considerations besides credit utilization when it comes to whether you should cancel or not cancel a credit card. Another reason not to cancel is that you need a healthy mix of types of credit accounts. If you cancel your only credit card, that would leave you deficient in the revolving credit category. Canceling a credit card that you've had open for a long time also reduces the length of your credit history, which is could be an additional injury to your credit score.

MANAGE YOUR CREDIT SCORE

We've just been talking about your credit score, but what exactly is it and why does it matter? And what does it have to do with debt? Managing your credit score is actually a secret to reducing and eliminating debt. Your credit score is how all creditors, such as home lenders and credit card companies, judge your ability to repay your debts. High credit scores are better than low scores. Someone with a high credit score is deemed to be less risky than someone with a low score. The better your credit rating, the more favorable you appear to lenders, as well as to potential landlords, insurers, and even employers. A good credit score helps them quickly approve your applications and offer you the best credit and terms available, which can translate to paying less and saving more.

Your credit score has a somewhat secret life because it's changing and being manipulated by your financial decisions even though it's out of sight. But you need to be mindful of the underground credit world and take the mystery away by pulling back the veil as often as you can. The Federal Fair Credit Reporting Act (FCRA) allows you to get your credit reports from each of the three major credit bureaus—Equifax, TransUnion, and Experian—for free once a year. The best strategy is to space them out, so you get a report from a different bureau every four months. Put it on your calendar to go to annualcreditreport.com, where you can view or download each of your reports annually. Look for any incorrect personal or credit information and be sure to dispute it with the bureau right away. You'll notice that your free credit reports don't reveal your actual credit score; unfortunately, you have to pay for those.

Each agency has its own method for calculating credit scores, but they've been fairly standardized. Most are based on the most widely used credit score—the Fair Isaac Corporation or FICO—which ranges from 300 to 850. You can purchase your score from the individual bureau Web sites or from myfico.com. You don't need to buy your score from each one, especially if all your free credit reports look about the same.

Five Factors That Determine Credit Score

It's great to be aware of what's on your credit report, but how do you actually manage it? According to myfico.com there are five major factors that determine credit score for the average person. If you have very little credit, not all of these factors may influence your score in the exact percentages listed.

1. **Payment history = 35 percent of your credit score.** That's the highest factor percentage, which means it's critical to pay all your bills on time. Your payment history influences your credit score the most. Having the following on your report will significantly lower your score:

- Bankruptcy
- Judgments
- Lawsuits
- Liens
- Wage garnishments
- Collection/delinquency items

2. **Amounts owed = 30 percent of your credit score.** The number of accounts you have with balances and the amounts you owe on them is the second highest credit score factor. Your "credit utilization" makes up the majority of this credit variable. Credit utilization is also called the debt to credit ratio. It's the ratio of your credit balances to your credit limits. Here's how it's figured:

> If you have a credit card with a $4,000 credit limit and you owe $1,000, you're using 25 percent of your available credit. To calculate your credit utilization for any credit account, divide your current balance by the credit limit: $1,000 ÷ $4,000 = 0.25 or 25 percent.

Never max out all your available credit lines, even if you pay off your balance in full each month. Instead, keep a good cushion of available credit. A safe guideline is to never let your balance exceed 30 percent of your credit limit. There's no specific ratio that FICO or the credit bureaus recommend, but the lower you keep your credit utilization, the better.

Keeping a sufficient gap between your current balance and your available credit line shows lenders that you're not the type to over-extend yourself. It's better to have two credit cards that each have balances below 30 percent of your credit limits than to have one card that you consistently max out. Another strategy is to apply for a credit limit increase. (I only recommend this if you use credit cards responsibly.) Call the company or complete an online credit request at their Web site. If you've been a good-paying customer, the creditor may accommodate you. The higher your credit limit with the major credit cards, the more likely potential lenders will be to extend you credit as well. And a higher limit also helps you maintain a larger credit cushion.

3. **Length of credit history = 15 percent of your credit score.** This credit factor means that you need to build up a sufficient credit history to increase your score. If you have credit card accounts that you don't use anymore, consider keeping them open, since the length of time that you have credit history is important. I recommend having at least one major credit card account in good standing to show that you're responsible with money. I know that I've discouraged you from using credit cards because they're so easy to abuse. But if you occasionally make a small charge and pay the bill off in full each month, you can slowly improve your credit rating. That will also prevent your card issuer from canceling your account due to inactivity.

4. **New credit = 10 percent of your credit score.** The number of recently opened accounts and recent credit inquiries plays a role in reducing your score. Don't apply for new retail charge cards or any additional accounts unless it's absolutely necessary. Many stores try to entice you to open a new credit account by offering discounts and promotions on your first credit purchase. Lots of inquiries make you appear too impulsive or eager for new credit.

5. **Types of credit used = 10 percent of your credit score.** The number and types of accounts, such as credit cards, auto loans, mortgages, home equity lines of credit, and retail accounts affect your score. Having a mix of various credit accounts positively affects your score.

DEBT SETTLEMENT

Now that you know how to use credit cards wisely, let's get back to getting out of debt. If you've paid down as many debts as possible with your existing assets and made attempts to lower your monthly obligations, you may still find that your debts are unmanageable. Here's a quick and dirty tip many people don't know about: You can often settle a debt for less than you owe. If you have legitimate debts that are in default (which means you've missed payment due dates), you should contact those creditors or collection agencies directly. It's been my experience that people who communicate quickly and honestly with creditors can get favorable treatment from them. I know that might sound daunting, but I promise that it can be easier than you think. Many creditors are willing to reduce your debt significantly in order to get some amount of payment from you right away. The potential savings you can realize from negotiating a debt settlement is just too important to your financial health not to try it. If you can pay a token amount immediately or make a larger lump sum payment fairly soon, you're in a good position to negotiate with your creditors. The best debts to negotiate are unsecured debts, because they aren't backed by assets that the lender could sell. These might include credit card and medical bills, for example.

DO YOU HAVE CREDIT INSURANCE?

Before you contact your creditors, check to see if you purchased or are currently paying for credit insurance. Credit insurance pays off a debt when certain situations occur, such as the loss of a family member who was providing income, or the loss of your job. You may have been sold credit insurance as part of getting a loan and not even be aware of it. If you're paying credit insurance premiums, they'll be itemized on your loan or credit card statements. If so, request a copy of the policy and see if it applies to your current situation.

Contact Creditors

Never be intimidated or afraid to contact a creditor. They'll usually respond more kindly than you think they will. That's because the vast majority of people in debt try to hide from creditors instead of deciding to address their problems head on. When you call, simply ask to speak to the collections department or to a debt counselor. Be polite but firm and clear about the fact that you're contacting them in an effort to settle or modify an outstanding debt. Don't get emotional. Remember that it's a business conversation for the person on the other end of the line. Be truthful about your situation, then let them do the talking. Be sure to have a pencil and paper handy to take notes. Write down the creditor or agency name, the date and time, the first and last name of the person you speak to, their direct phone number, and anything important they say.

If they tell you right away that you can not settle your debt for less than the full amount, know that they're probably just negotiating with you, especially if the debt is old. Understand that it's extremely likely that they will take less money than they indicate. Let them know if you're in the process of speaking with other creditors and that you really want to work something out with them. Offer to pay 25 percent of the amount of the full debt that you owe. Perhaps they'll meet you in the middle at 50 percent of your debt. Many credit card companies would be thrilled to get half of your debt right away rather than zero down the road. But if they won't budge, don't seem too desperate to settle; try calling them back in a few days. It's likely that you'll speak to a different representative who may see the situation differently. If after several attempts they won't reduce the original debt amount, try requesting that all fees and interest be waived from the account. Always get revised terms on your debt in writing from the creditor or collections agency before you make any payments to them. Be sure to make settlement payments with a cashier's check or money order, never with cash or a personal check. That ensures you don't reveal your bank account information and gives you proof of payment.

Sick of Medical Debt?

Medical debt presents some special problems because the billing and insurance system is so complicated. When you can't read or understand the lingo on a medical bill, it's easy for insurance mistakes to occur and for fraud to go unnoticed. The Medical Billing Advocates of America at billadvocates.com may be able to help you verify the accuracy of any medical bills that you don't understand. They also offer advice on negotiating settlements with hospitals or other medical providers. Generally you should approach negotiations for medical bills the same way as for other types of debt: Make an offer to pay off a percentage of your outstanding debt as quickly as you can. As tempting as it may be to pay overdue medical bills with a credit card, resist the temptation. That's because creditors are likely to view medical debt with more sympathy than credit card debt. They may be more willing to work out a favorable payment plan for debt that's due to unforeseen medical problems versus for debt they assume to be the result of frivolous spending.

Get Free of Legal Debts

For legal debts related to a judgment against you or one already being garnished from your wages, try requesting a modified garnishment. If you're already behind on child support, you need to pull out all the stops to get caught up, even by taking an advance on a credit card. That's because going to jail is just about the best way to escalate any debt problem! If you have a debt owed to the IRS, it's best to contact the Taxpayer Advocate Service to discuss your best options, instead of ignoring a bill from Uncle Sam. They may give you an "offer in compromise," which is similar to a debt settlement, or an extended payment agreement. Go to irs.gov for more information about ways to resolve tax delinquencies.

 Here's a quick and dirty tip: If you have medical debt, ask about hospital medical assistance funds and do some research at the Centers for Medicare and Medicaid Services at cms.hhs.gov.

Dealing with Debt Professionals

Debt negotiators are representatives who aggressively work with your creditors. Many claim to be able to reduce debts by 50 percent or more, but they usually charge a big fee to do it. You aren't required to have anyone else negotiate on your behalf. You can do exactly what they do, perhaps even better in some cases. But if you choose to work with a debt negotiator, look for one that's certified by the International Association of Professional Debt Arbitrators (iapda.org) and review their fee schedules and contracts very closely. Or you may choose to hire an attorney to negotiate verbally or in writing for you.

There are also debt settlement agencies that offer debt management plans (DMPs). DMPs are also called one-pay plans because the agency collects one monthly payment from you. They distribute the money to your creditors after negotiating lower payments on your behalf. If you enroll in a DMP, protect yourself by confirming the plan directly with your creditors. Don't send any payments to a third-party company until you know the plan is legitimate. To learn more about DMPs, go to the Federal Trade Commission Web site at ftc.gov and click on the "consumer protection" tab.

LOAN REFINANCING

Now that we've talked about ways to optimize and settle your debts, let's get into some more specific strategies to reduce debts. Most types of loans—for houses, cars, and education, for example—have the potential to be refinanced. Doing a refinance means your old loan is paid off and a new loan is created. It's a powerful tool that can be used to your benefit in a variety of situations. I'll just refer to mortgage refinances in this section, since they're the most common type. Your eligibility to refinance is similar to the approval process you went through to get your original loan. The lender will verify your income, debts, credit score, property value, and more. If your credit rating has improved since the time you took the original loan, that will help you get the lowest interest rate possible.

Here are five reasons you may want to refinance a loan:

1. To convert to a fixed-rate loan
2. To lock in a lower interest rate
3. To lower your monthly payments
4. To manage a balloon payment
5. To cash out equity you've built up

Each of these reasons makes sense in the right situation and I'll review them all. But first, there are some basic concepts you need to know about refinancing. It's important to understand that refinancing a loan can be expensive. Even mortgages that are advertised as being "no-cost" or "low-cost" always have fees hidden somewhere. Anytime you get a new loan there are fees that have to be paid to the lender as well as to other parties involved in the transaction. You must carefully weigh the total costs against the long-term savings or benefits you'd receive from doing a refinance. Typical closing costs for a refinance could be as high as 3 percent to 5 percent of the outstanding loan amount or more. Fees vary depending on the location of the property and the lender, but should be similar to or less than the costs you paid for the original loan. You may be able to finance your closing costs by adding them to your new loan amount. However, when you "roll" closing costs into a loan, not only does the amount you borrow increase, but so may the interest rate you pay for the life of the loan. For that reason, it's best to pay loan closing costs up front when you can, instead of borrowing them.

If you plan to refinance, it's best to start by contacting your current lender. They'll probably want to keep your business and may be willing to give you a favorable interest rate or to eliminate some of the typical refinancing fees like the application or origination

Here's a quick and dirty tip: Always evaluate the long-term savings you can get by paying loan closing costs up front. Ask the lender for a side-by-side comparison of principal loan balances, interest rates, and monthly payments for each loan option.

fee. In chapter 8, I'll cover much more about mortgages and real estate closing costs.

Calculate Your Loan-to-Value Ratio

To refinance, you must have a loan-to-value (LTV) ratio that falls within the lender's guidelines. What's an acceptable LTV ratio varies from lender to lender. They'll require a new or fairly recent appraisal of your property to make their calculation. Here's how to estimate your LTV:

1. Find out how much your property is approximately worth (Zillow.com can help)
2. Find out how much you currently owe on the property
3. Divide the loan amount (#2) by the value amount (#1)

Here's an example to consider:

Amy and Alan want to refinance their $250,000 mortgage on their vacation river house to take advantage of reduced interest rates. Their lender requires an LTV that does not exceed 80 percent to do a refinance. The market value of their property is estimated to be $300,000. So their LTV is $250,000 divided by $300,000, which equals 83 percent. Unfortunately that exceeds the lender's 80 percent LTV requirement and their refinance application is denied.

To know if the cost of doing a refinance is worth it, you need to know the financial break-even point (BEP). A refinance BEP occurs when you fully recover your costs and start to benefit from the refinance. The BEP depends on various factors such as the old and new loan interest rates, closing costs, your income tax bracket, how

---

Here's a quick and dirty tip: Use the Refinance Breakeven Calculator at dinkytown.com to determine if refinancing makes sense for your situation.

long you plan to own the home, and any loan prepayment penalties you have to pay. If you sell the property prior to reaching the BEP, there's no benefit to doing a refinance because you'd spend more than you'd save.

Let's get back to the five reasons you might consider doing a refinance:

1. **Convert to a fixed-rate loan.** A fixed-rate loan gives you a predictable monthly payment that can't increase. That's different from how other types of mortgages work, such as the adjustable-rate and interest-only mortgage. Non-fixed-rate loan payments can increase when interest rates go up, which means you pay more interest on the balance of what you owe. A fixed-rate loan may have a larger monthly payment than other options; however, it can still save you a bundle in interest over the life of the loan. Have a lender do a side-by-side comparison for you, so you can compare total costs.

2. **Lock in a lower interest rate.** If you find that the interest rate for your type of loan has dropped, you should always run the break-even numbers for doing a refinance. Take the time to investigate the potential benefits of refinancing any long-term installment loan when interest rates are decreasing. Sometimes we get fooled into thinking that small changes in interest rates aren't worth the hassle of doing a refinance. A good rule of thumb is to investigate doing a refinance whenever the interest rates have dipped approximately 1 percent below your current rate. Here's an example to help you see how small changes in interest rates can make a huge difference over the life of a long-term loan such as a mortgage:

> Sarah bought a house for $200,000 with a 5 percent down payment. She put $10,000 down and mortgaged the remaining $190,000. Her loan is to be repaid over thirty years at a 6.75 percent fixed rate of interest. That means she'll pay a whopping $253,641 just in interest over the life of the mortgage! That doesn't even include the $190,000 in principal she has to repay. If interest rates for thirty-year fixed rate mortgages go down to 6 percent from 6.75 percent, should Sarah consider doing a refinance? Let's see . . .

If Sarah refinanced the loan for thirty years at the new interest rate of 6 percent, by comparison she'd pay $220,092 in interest. That's a savings of $33,549 in interest over the life of a thirty-year loan. The "refi" would reduce her monthly payment from $1,232 to $1,139, giving her a monthly savings of $93. At first glance a savings of $93 per month seems great, but as I mentioned, doing a refinance also costs money. I used the Refinance Breakeven Calculator at dinkytown.com to enter basic information from the example about Sarah. With closing costs equal to 3 percent of the $190,000 loan balance, she would need to keep her refinanced loan for approximately five years to break even and make the refinance worthwhile.

3. **Lower your monthly payments.** A common goal of refinancing is to save money with lower monthly payments. The lender does that by extending the maturity date of the debt, reducing the interest rate, or both. A good strategy for the savings you might receive from doing a refinance is to use it to make extra payments on your highest interest (most expensive) debt and pay it down faster. You must be clear about what you're trying to accomplish from doing a refinance and carefully weigh the pros and cons. If you run a breakeven calculation and find that the long-term savings will offset the costs related to a refinance, it's probably worthwhile. If you can put the savings to good use or can invest the savings wisely, you'll come out ahead.

The following chart shows variations on a $150,000 mortgage:

TERM	INTEREST RATE	MONTHLY PAYMENT	TOTAL INTEREST PAID
30 years	5%	$805	$139,883
30 years	6%	$899	$173,757
30 years	7%	$998	$209,263
15 years	5%	$1,186	$63,514
15 years	6%	$1,265	$77,841
15 years	7%	$1,348	$92,683

4. **To manage a balloon payment.** A balloon payment is a large payment that's due at the end of a loan. For example, you might borrow $300,000, but have monthly payments based on just $100,000 for a ten-year period. The remaining $200,000 would be due as a final payment to the lender at the end of the ten-year term. Since most borrowers don't have the ability to fully pay off a large balloon payment, they choose to refinance.

5. **To cash out equity you've built up.** Taking equity out of a home by doing a refinance can be a bad idea if you spend it on a Caribbean vacation. Squandering equity on anything that won't increase your net worth is detrimental to your financial health. But cashing out equity can be a smart idea if you use the money for an alternate investment that appreciates in value or will make you more money than you have to pay in interest. Follow this example about a real estate investor:

> John has a rental property worth $150,000 and he owes $100,000 on the mortgage. That means he has equity of $50,000. Let's say he refinances 80 percent of the property's market value, which is $120,000 ($150,000×0.80). His closing costs total $4,500 and will be rolled into the new loan. That's a new loan of $124,500 ($120,000+$4,500). John gets to pocket the difference between his new loan and his old one: $24,000 ($124,000-$100,000). If he can invest the $24,000 for a better return than what he has to pay in interest for the refinanced loan, he'll come out ahead. For instance, if his interest rate on the loan is 7 percent and he puts the $24,000 down on the purchase of a rental property that will yield him a total return of 10 percent, the refinance is worth it. However, it's an investment risk that shouldn't be entered into lightly.

Here's a quick and dirty tip: To qualify for a mortgage refinance, lenders may insist that your property not be for sale within the last six months. If they believe your plan is to sell the property in the near future, that scenario would make doing a refinance less profitable for them.

LOAN MODIFICATION

Before you decide to embark on a mortgage refinance, I highly recommend that you approach your current lender about doing a loan modification. A modification is basically a refinance that's both easy and free. The lender can reduce your loan payment by extending the maturity date, reducing the interest rate, or by doing both. A loan modification can also help when a lender adds any past due amounts to the principal loan balance or offers forbearance, which is a temporary suspension of monthly payments.

The Home Affordable Modification Program (HAMP) is a government program available to participating lenders until December 31, 2012. It allows lenders to lower a borrower's monthly payment to as low as 31 percent of their gross (pretax) monthly income. If your income has been substantially reduced or if you don't have funds available to do a typical refinance, you may be a perfect candidate for a modification. Home owners who are behind in making mortgage payments or who demonstrate they are close to default are qualified for the government's modification program. However, you must prove that you have adequate income to afford a reduced payment going forward. You may be obligated to prove that you can make the modified payment during a three-month trial period before the modification is finalized. The mortgage must have been originated before January 1, 2009, and must be for your primary residence. Visit makinghomeaffordable.gov and financialstability.gov for current program information. Or contact your lender to find out if they offer this free program—all lending institutions who accepted economic stimulus funds are required to participate.

LOAN MODIFICATION SCAMS

There have been some scams associated with loan modifications. Be wary of paying an individual or a company who promises to work with your lender to modify your loan. That's something you should be able to do yourself with a phone call to the lender. If you work with a credit counselor or consultant, always get a written contract from them that describes in detail what they're going to do for you before you make any payments. The following Web sites are good anti-fraud resources:

- occ.treas.gov
- ftc.gov
- fdic.gov/consumers

If you don't qualify for a modification, and have anything other than a conventional 15- or 30-year fixed-rate mortgage, it's in your best interest to contact a couple of different lenders about your options. Everyone's situation is different and the loan market is always changing. A good lender or mortgage broker should be able to make some suggestions for your circumstances. You can do some preliminary research at one of my favorite Web sites, bankrate.com. You'll find calculators there for just about every situation and type of mortgage product that you may have.

LOAN OR DEBT CONSOLIDATION

Another way to save money on monthly payments for loans or credit card debt is to consider a loan consolidation. A consolidation allows you to lump together two or more debts into one new, larger loan. The lender pays off your existing loan or debt balances and replaces them with a single loan, so you have just one lender to pay. Consolidation can be done for credit card debt and many different types of loans such as mortgages, home equity lines of credit (HELOCs), auto, and student loans. A consolidation is useful if you need to lower your monthly debt obligation. But many times lenders accomplish the monthly savings by stretching out the term of the loan, not by lowering your average interest rate. If your existing loans are at relatively high interest rates, getting a consolidation loan at a lower average rate can save you a large amount of interest over time. Otherwise, the consolidation loan will lower your monthly payment but cost you more in interest over the life of the loan.

Loan consolidations can be risky for lenders; therefore they're becoming less common financing options. If a debtor is having trouble meeting their monthly obligations and has poor credit, a lender will be wary of extending them a large loan that could go into default. However, federal student loans are commonly consolidated because they're a low-risk debt that's almost certain to be repaid. That's because the government can use its full power to get payment from you—not even a bankruptcy can discharge a federal student loan. I'll discuss more about student loans and paying for education in chapter 9.

Consolidating Student Loans

I frequently get questions from *Money Girl* podcast listeners and blog readers who have multiple student loans and don't know what to do with them. Both students and parents can consolidate education loans; however, they can't combine loans that are in different names. Only loans from the same borrower can be consolidated—even married couples must keep their respective education loans separate. There are usually minimal fees to do a student loan consolidation and you can work with any lender you choose. Most federal student loans can be consolidated, but finding lenders that will consolidate private student loans is more difficult. In general, private student loans can not be consolidated with federal loans. Approval for a private student loan consolidation will depend on your credit score. If you've graduated and have been building a good credit history, an improved score may qualify you for a lower interest rate. Start by speaking with your current lender(s) and ask if they'll reduce

Here's a quick and dirty tip: Finaid.org has a list of federal and private student loan institutions, including lenders that specifically offer consolidation loans. You can also get a consolidation loan directly from the U.S. Department of Education at loanconsolidation.ed.gov.

your interest rate(s). They may be willing to do that rather than lose your business to another lender.

For federal student loan consolidations, consider any special features of your original loans that are important to you. Benefits such as forgiveness for public service work, forbearance for financial hardship, and certain interest rate discounts and rebates might be lost with a student loan consolidation. So be sure to ask potential lenders about loan options that you'd be forced to give up in doing a consolidation. With some federal student loans, it's possible to get the benefits of flexible repayment options, such as extended or graduated payments, without doing a consolidation. Use the Loan Consolidation Calculator at finaid.org to compare the monthly savings to the increase in total interest expense over the life of the loan. Carefully analyze the cost of repaying your original loans against the cost of paying for a consolidated loan.

SECRET DEBT WEAPON: ACCELERATED PAYMENTS

There's a secret weapon you can use to whittle down your principle balance on loans faster and pay less interest without paying a dime. It's so simple you may not believe me: Make biweekly payments instead of monthly payments. You normally don't have to arrange this with your lender. Accelerated payments work for all types of installment loans and mortgages, as long as there isn't an expensive prepayment penalty. When you understand how much you can save by making biweekly payments, you'll want to jump for joy each time you send the payment in!

Here's an example to demonstrate how the biweekly payment weapon works:

Christine's fixed-rate mortgage is $158,250 to be repaid over thirty years at a 6.5 percent rate of interest. Her payment is $1,000 per month, or $12,000 per year. If she keeps that payment schedule, over the life of the loan she'll pay a total of $201,838 in interest. On the other hand, if she makes biweekly payments, she pays half the monthly payment, or $500, every other week. That means she pays a total of $13,000 each year instead of $12,000. Keeping a biweekly schedule will reduce Christine's interest expense from $201,838 to $184,122. That's a serious savings of $17,716! Not to mention that she'd pay off the loan in just over twenty-seven years instead of in thirty years.

Biweekly payments aren't really magic; they simply take advantage of the fact that one month out of each quarter has five weeks in it, instead of four. There are thirteen weeks in each quarter, not twelve; and there are fifty-two weeks in a year, not forty-eight. So it's a sneaky way to get the equivalent of one extra monthly payment made each year. That additional amount works wonders toward paying down a loan faster, which means you pay a lot less interest over time. The method works especially well if you get paid every other week, so you can budget the biweekly loan payment to occur close to each payday. And it's not just for mortgage payments—you can use the biweekly weapon for any installment debt, like car and student loans, too.

This chart shows more examples of the potential savings from making biweekly loan payments:

LOAN TERMS	MONTHLY P & I PAYMENT	TOTAL INTEREST PAID	VS.	BIWEEKLY P & I PAYMENT	TOTAL INTEREST PAID	REDUCED PAY-OFF TIME	TOTAL INTEREST SAVINGS
$190,000 30 years 6% interest	$1,139	$220,090		$569.50	$201,795	Paid off in 27.3 years	**$18,295**
$150,000 30 years 6% interest	$899	$173,755		$449	$159,311	Paid off in 27.3 years	**$14,444**
$300,000 30 years 7% interest	$1,996	$418,524		$998	$379,023	Paid off in 27 years	**$38,501**

Another way to pay down a loan even faster and get significant interest savings is to send extra principal-only payments. Of course, the more you pay down your principal balance, the more interest you save—but even paying an extra $50 per month can

Here's a quick and dirty tip: Never pay a lender a fee to make accelerated payments—that's a scam! Unless your loan includes a prepayment penalty, you are free to make extra payments or to pay it off early.

make a huge difference. Take the same loan example from above for $158,250 at 6.5 percent interest to be repaid over thirty years. If Christine sends an extra $50 each month with the original payment of $1,000, the additional payment allows her to pay off the loan in just over twenty-six years and saves her $30,789 in interest.

A LAST RESORT: DECLARING BANKRUPTCY

If you're seriously drowning in debt, the option of last resort is to declare bankruptcy. Because a bankruptcy can stay on your credit report for up to ten years, it will affect many aspects of your financial life for a long time. There are strict requirements to qualify for relief under any type of bankruptcy. Filing is a complex process that costs money and usually requires the guidance of a specialized attorney. The most common types of bankruptcy for individuals are Chapter 7 and Chapter 13.

With Chapter 7 bankruptcy, some debts can be completely eliminated or discharged, and others can not. Those that won't go away include judgments, child support, alimony, tax bills, federal student loans, and secured debts such as mortgages. Chapter 7 is generally the best option for those who have little property but a lot of unsecured debt such as credit card or medical bills.

Chapter 13 bankruptcy is very different because it doesn't eliminate any debts, but restructures them. It's also known as a wage earner's plan because it follows a court-approved repayment schedule. That delays and reduces payments to all creditors, including mortgage lenders and the IRS, as long as the agreed-upon payment plan is honored by the debtor.

If you're considering filing bankruptcy, you should consult a bankruptcy attorney for help with making some tough decisions.

But first, anyone who intends to declare bankruptcy must get pre-filing credit counseling from an approved agency within six months before the filing. The agency must be approved by the U.S. Department of Justice in the judicial district where you plan to file bankruptcy. To find the approved agencies, do a search at usdoj.gov.

Even if you're not considering bankruptcy, but have a debt problem that's gotten out of control, you can contact a credit counselor for guidance. Ignoring a financial problem can only make matters worse. You'll want to seek out a nonprofit credit counseling agency that gets most of its funding from your creditors, not from you. They may require nominal fees, but won't try to sell you anything. Make sure to choose a company that's accredited with an industry agency such as the National Foundation for Credit Counseling (nfcc.org) or the Association of Independent Consumer Credit Counseling Agencies (aiccca.org).

An organization that provides support and guidance to those with serious debt and spending addictions is Debtors Anonymous. Their stated mission is to help compulsive debtors stop incurring unsecured debt. There are no fees or dues for membership, nor are they aligned with any religious or political institution. You can take a debt quiz on their Web site at debtorsanonymous.org that may reveal if you have a compulsive debt problem.

SET YOUR DEBT PRIORITIES

Thinking about debt and how to get out of it can be depressing. Many people are overwhelmed by their financial obligations and feel trapped. I want to offer some words of encouragement if you're struggling with any amount of debt. The best way to overcome a challenge is to meet it head on. You can unbury yourself. Successful people stay focused on finding solutions, not dwelling on their problems.

One of the questions I often hear about getting out and staying out of debt has to do with setting priorities. You may be confused or feel conflicted about what to do with your discretionary income. You know you need to pay down debt and put money toward your other goals, like saving for retirement and an emergency fund. Your priorities for doing those should depend on your situation. If you have no emergency fund, your top priority should be to build up at least a couple thousand dollars. One of the ways you can get sucked into short-term debt is by getting caught without an emergency fund. Having a cash reserve is a fundamental part of being financially healthy. (And never, ever dip into it for anything other than a critical emergency.) It's important to expect the unexpected, because life throws lots of expensive mishaps at us. Cars break down, people get sick, and jobs can be lost. In many cases, those types of problems may be the reason you got into debt in the first place. Don't let it happen again.

Once you have your emergency fund in place, you can start paying down your short-term debts. If you have a retirement plan at work that offers company matching (more about that to come), I recommend that you continue to contribute to it while you reduce your dangerous short-term debts like credit cards or payday loans. If you have a large amount of short-term debt and don't have a workplace retirement plan that offers matching funds, I recommend that you spend six months to a year working exclusively and diligently to pay down your debt. Put retirement savings on hold for a specific time frame, so you can send as much money as possible to your most dangerous, high-priority debts. After that time period, begin saving for retirement while you continue to pay down short-term, then long-term debt. But if your short-term debt is manageable, I don't recommend that you stop saving for retirement. As important as it is to get out of debt, you must also have a plan for a financially secure future.

Just like losing a lot of weight doesn't happen overnight, getting out of debt won't happen quickly, either. It's a part of making a commitment to a new and improved lifestyle. It's a part of accepting new beliefs about money and adopting better financial habits that you follow every day. Don't let the desperation you may feel about your situation allow you to fall prey to get-out-of-debt-quick scams. Even those created by so-called nonprofits, who claim to have your best interests at heart, may not be legitimate. You'll conquer your debt by being persistent and chipping away at it bit by bit.

Make a commitment to work proactively to improve your financial health every day. Spend your time and energy on a good strategy and create systems that will help you climb out of a financial hole, not slide back in it. Stay on top of your net worth—update your Personal Financial Statement frequently to monitor your progress and see your big financial picture. Put your full attention on these solutions:

- Increase your income
- Decrease your fixed and variable expenses
- Increase your savings and the interest rate you receive on it
- Increase your investments and the rate of return you receive on them
- Reorganize and optimize your debts so they cost you less by refinancing, modifying, consolidating, or using balance transfer cards when it's prudent
- Negotiate for debt settlements when possible
- Pay down your debts starting with the most dangerous and expensive ones
- Automate your savings and extra debt payments so they're paid first
- Create long-term financial goals that motivate you
- Simplify your lifestyle

Become the master of your money. Make a decision that you're going to control it, and not let it control you. Manage it wisely and make smart moves and you'll create a richer, more secure future for yourself and your family.

6

Investing Wisely

If you would be wealthy, think of saving as well as getting.
—BENJAMIN FRANKLIN

In order to reach some of your long-term goals that we talked about earlier—like having enough money for retirement—you have to invest. The fact that investing money means you could possibly lose money makes it a scary proposition for many people. No one can know for sure what an investment in a stock, a mutual fund, or a parcel of real estate, for example, will yield in the future. Financial analysts make forecasts based on what happened in the past filtered by the current economic climate. The investment disclaimer you hear always reads, "Past performance does not guarantee future results." What that means is that no matter how smart or lucky an analyst is, they can't predict the future with 100% certainty.

Successful investors learn how to minimize risk using techniques that we'll cover in this chapter, such as asset allocation, diversification, and dollar-cost averaging. I'll tell you what you need to know to create a strategy for making wise investments. You'll learn key investing concepts, get to know all the different investment vehicles to choose from, and see how easy it is to limit investment risk—no matter what's going on in the financial markets. Let's start by covering some fundamental investing lingo and concepts.

DISCRETIONARY INCOME: YOUR INVESTMENT FUEL

The most basic concept to hold dear when it comes to building wealth is that you need discretionary income in order to save and invest for the future. Discretionary income is what you have left over at the end of the month after all your essential living expenses are paid. We discussed this in chapter 2; you remember, right? It comes from spending less than you make. I'm bringing it up again because it's so essential and powerful. Without it, you simply don't have the ability to save and invest, period. Money that you spend on most "stuff" is gone and can't be used as a resource to build wealth. Living paycheck to paycheck may take care of your immediate wants and needs, but it is dangerous because it leaves you vulnerable to unexpected hardships. If you never set aside money for emergencies or for your long-term needs, you're not financially grounded—you're simply drifting from one bank deposit to the next. Even well-paid professionals make the mistake of not being financially grounded. It's not uncommon for wealthy people to overextend themselves with homes, cars, clothes, and high-priced toys that they think other people expect them to have as part of their upscale image. The trade-off for those temporary luxuries may be a future without financial security.

The first step to having discretionary income is to secure your ability to create income from a job, a business, freelance work, or a combination of endeavors. I know that probably seems obvious; however, many people don't protect their ability to make money or attempt to find additional sources of income. I'm not suggesting that you work three jobs if you really don't need to. But I challenge you to question how secure your current income really is and to be open to new and creative ways to make money.

Here's a quick and dirty tip: Read Robert Allen's *Multiple Streams of Income: How to Generate a Lifetime of Unlimited Wealth!* This book will open your mind to the many ways you can create new sources of income.

One word of advice about increasing your income: It'll become increasingly tempting to spend it! Try not to let your expenses increase as your income grows—that's what I call the "potted plant syndrome." When you put a plant in a bigger pot, it will naturally expand and use more of the pot's soil and resources. Don't use up all your newly found resources and let your living expenses match or exceed your income. Once you have additional income, your mission is to be incredibly diligent about ways to reduce your expenses at the same time. A growing income combined with shrinking expenses is a recipe for financial success, no matter how much you make.

HOW DO SIMPLE AND COMPOUND INTEREST WORK?

It's important to understand how your money actually earns interest. There are a couple different types of interest: simple interest and compound interest. Simple interest is pretty simple. It's only calculated on the original principal amount. Let's say you gave your best friend a loan of $1,000 at a 5 percent annual rate of simple interest for a term of three years. Here's the interest calculation for the loan:

Year #1: $1,000 × 5% = $50 interest due
Year #2: $1,000 × 5% = $50 interest due
Year #3: $1,000 × 5% = $50 interest due

At the end of the third year you would get back the principal amount of $1,000 and have earned an additional $150 in interest. Your $1,000 investment grew to $1,150.

Compound interest allows you to earn interest not only on your original amount but also on the interest you've accumulated over time. Compounding is the ability to make earnings on your earnings. When interest you earn on an investment is compounded, it grows at a much faster rate than with simple interest. And the more often interest gets added back to the principal, the better. For example, a savings account that pays 2 percent interest that's compounded daily, will give you more earnings than one that pays 2 percent compounded quarterly. Let's use the same example where you loan a friend $1,000 for three years. Here's how much you would earn if you charged 5 percent interest compounded annually:

Year #1: $1,000×5% = $50 interest due = $1,050 balance
Year #2: $1,050×5% = $52.50 interest due = $1,102.50 balance
Year #3: $1,102.50×5% = $55.13 interest due = $1,157.63 balance

At the end of the third year you would get back the principal amount of $1,000 and have earned an additional $157.63 in interest. Your $1,000 investment grew to $1,157.63.

Let's see how much you'd earn if you charged 5% compounded semi-annually:

Year #1: $1,000×2.5% = $25 interest due = $1,025 balance
           $1,025×2.5% = $25.63 interest due = $1,050.63 balance
Year #2: $1,050.63×2.5% = $25.27 interest due = $1,076.90 balance
           $1,076.90×2.5% = $26.92 interest due = $1,103.82 balance
Year #3: $1,103.82×2.5% = $27.60 interest due = $1,131.42 balance
           $1,131.42×2.5% = $28.29 interest due = $1,159.71 balance

At the end of the third year you would get back the principal amount of $1,000 and have earned an additional $159.71 in interest. Your $1,000 investment grew to $1,159.71 with semiannual compounding.

The more frequent the compounding, the more you can earn. If your money is compounded daily instead of quarterly, that results in a higher annual percentage yield (APY). For example, two CDs may pay the same interest rate but pay it on a different schedule. If one CD pays interest monthly and the other CD pays interest quarterly, and you roll the interest back into the account (instead of withdrawing it), you'll earn a higher APY from the product with monthly compounding because it's more frequent. The important point to remember is that as you hold an interest-bearing investment for a long period of time, compound interest results in dramatic earnings and growth.

THE TIME VALUE OF MONEY

There's a fundamental financial principle called the time value of money (TVM) that's important to consider when making financial decisions. TVM is the idea that money you could have today is worth more than the same amount you could have at any point in the future, due to its potential to earn interest. That's why if you ever win the lottery (go ahead, dream) you should receive the lump sum instead of getting the payout in future installments; the lump sum would allow you to earn interest on the entire amount right away.

INVESTING AND RISK

If there was no risk to getting a stellar return on your money, everyone would run to the highest-yielding investments. But high return investments usually bring higher risks. So investors walk a line between the desire to make money and the desire not to lose money. Risk is a relative concept that can only be gauged by each investor. Your risk tolerance has to do with how you react emotionally when your investments decline in value. Volatility is the amount of uncertainty related to changes in an investment's value. High volatility means that the price can go up or down dramatically in a short period of time. Low volatility means that an investment's price or value changes very little over a given period of time.

If temporary investment losses make you climb the walls with anxiety all day or lay awake with worry all night, you're probably somewhat risk-averse. That means you don't like risk even if it means you may be missing out on higher rates of return. On the other hand, if you stay cool as a cucumber and have confidence that your investments will bounce back over the time horizon that you have in mind, you're probably more suited to holding riskier investments,

such as stocks. Here's what you need to keep in mind when determining the amount of risk that's best for you:

- **Your age:** As you approach retirement age you should begin to
  take less financial risk and focus on preserving your wealth.
- **Your health:** If you're in poor health or are unable to work you
  should take fewer financial risks.
- **Your net worth:** If you have a high net worth you may feel
  comfortable making more aggressive, riskier investments than
  if you have a low net worth.
- **The number of additional years you'll earn income:** If you
  want to retire early you'll need to shift away from riskier investments and move to safer ones that provide fixed income,
  such as bonds or CDs.
- **The amount of future income you expect from inheritance,
  Social Security, or pensions, for example:** If you can count
  on receiving additional income in the future you may feel comfortable making riskier investments now.
- **Your investment goals and objectives:** If want to retire early
  or amass a huge nest egg, you'll need to be more aggressive and
  invest in higher-risk products, such as stock funds.

The money that you want to use for short-term goals, such as
savings for your emergency fund or for a car down payment, should
not be exposed to market volatility. That's because there's a real
possibility that an investment, such as a stock, could severely drop
in value at the moment you need it. Money you need for short-term
and even for some medium-term goals should be invested in a safe,
liquid account such as a savings or money market deposit account
at an FDIC-insured institution that can be converted into cash
quickly and conveniently.

However, funds you want to sock away for long-term needs (more
than ten years in the future) such as retirement or education usually
must be exposed to more risk in order to achieve higher returns that
will allow you to meet your goals. Investments in growth-oriented
stocks and stock funds will always demonstrate volatility, which is
exactly what makes them suitable for many investors' long-term

Here's a quick and dirty tip: Invest conservatively to achieve your short-term financial goals. That's because you have less time to recover from potential investment losses.

objectives. The bottom line is that you should never expose your money to more risk than is absolutely necessary to accomplish your goals. So it's important to be clear about when you'll need the money you plan to invest, because that determines how you should invest it.

THE DIFFERENCE BETWEEN SAVING AND INVESTING

Even though we tend to use the terms saving and investing interchangeably, they're not the same thing. The difference between the two has to do with taking financial risk. The purpose of saving money is to keep it safe and free from risk so you'll have it for emergencies and planned short-term purchases. As we've discussed, your emergency fund is an example of money that should always be saved in an FDIC-insured savings account. The purpose of investing money is to increase your net worth and to achieve large, long-term financial goals. Investing involves risk—the potential to lose money as well as the potential to make money.

WHAT'S THE SECURITIES INVESTOR'S PROTECTION CORPORATION?

Investments, or securities, are not insured by the FDIC because their value can fluctuate wildly. There's a nongovernment entity called the Securities Investors Protection Corporation (SIPC) that offers consumer protection for investments. They do not insure or guarantee investment funds that are lost. However, they do step in when brokerages fail or fraud is the cause of investor loss. The goal of the SIPC is to replace missing securities up to $500,000 per customer, including a maximum of $250,000 for cash losses. Find out more details at sipc.org.

Here's a quick and dirty tip: If you choose to invest conservatively for your long-term savings goals, you'll need to invest more money to offset potential inflation and the lower returns that conservative investments bring.

So whether you should save money or invest it depends on your time horizon—that's the amount of time between now and when you'll actually spend the money. If you're thirty and are investing to retire at age sixty-five, you have a very long thirty-five-year time horizon and you'll want to invest. But if it's January and you're saving money for your upcoming summer vacation, you have a very short six-month time horizon and you'll just want to save your money. Use the following chart as a guideline for the best types of accounts and investments for short, medium, and long-term goals. You'll notice that under the short-term goals column, there is no suitable investment type listed because money for short-term needs should never be exposed to risk. Don't worry if you're not familiar with some of the terms and information on this chart—we'll cover all of it.

	SHORT-TERM GOALS	MEDIUM-TERM GOALS	LONG-TERM GOALS
Years to accomplish	1	2 to 10	10 or more
Risk level	Low	Low to moderate	Moderate
Asset class	Cash	Cash, bonds, stocks	Bonds, stocks, real estate, commodities
Account types	Savings, money market deposit account, checking	CDs, 529 plan, Coverdell account, brokerage account	Retirement account, 529 plan, Coverdell, brokerage account

	SHORT-TERM GOALS	MEDIUM-TERM GOALS	LONG-TERM GOALS
Investment types	None	Treasuries, bond funds, conservative stock mutual funds and EFTs	Stock funds, growth mutual funds and ETFs, income funds, target-date funds, high-yield bond funds, real estate, commodity funds

WHAT INVESTMENTS SHOULD YOU BUY?

Now you know why investing is important, but how do you get started? There are so many ways to invest, which is fantastic, but it can also be very confusing to decide where to put your money. Don't let the variety of options give you analysis paralysis—that's what happens when you become intimidated or overwhelmed by lots of information. The stress of having to make a decision about investing can cause some people to retreat and do absolutely nothing. I'm going to help you determine what investment choices are right for you. Let's start by reviewing the various ways you can invest.

Stocks

Stocks are one of the most basic investments. Stocks are issued to the public by companies who want to raise funds. When you buy shares of stock, you're buying a small piece of ownership in a company that can go up or down in value over time. The terms equity, shares, and stock all mean the same thing. If a company is profitable enough to offer dividends to its shareholders, you'll be eligible to receive those on a per-share basis or to have them reinvested (that's how it works with retirement accounts). Stocks are primarily bought and sold in marketplaces called exchanges. You've probably heard of the New York Stock Exchange or the NASDAQ, for example.

Those are U.S. exchanges where buyers and sellers come together to primarily trade stocks.

Even though stocks are fundamentally simple investments, there are many thousands to choose from. Knowing which stocks will perform in the long or short term is difficult. Stock analysts continually watch the markets to find potential winners. There is a great deal of risk involved in investing in individual stocks. The price per share can be extremely volatile depending on the industry and how the stock market performs as a whole. Prices can skyrocket or plummet in a short period of time, which is why stocks are considered one of the riskiest asset classes.

You can easily invest money in individual stocks in a retirement account or regular brokerage account by using a traditional stockbroker or an online brokerage. Once you buy a stock, you can sell it for a profit or a loss at any time. Workplace retirement plans may offer a menu of stock mutual funds rather than individual stock purchases.

Bonds

Bonds are another type of investment available for your portfolio. A bond is very different from a stock. It's a form of debt—but not a form of debt that you owe! A bond is a loan that you give to the issuer with specific terms for repayment. The bond issuer could be a government entity or a corporation that wants to raise money for a specific project. You may have heard of municipal bonds, or "munis," which are issued by a municipality, state, or county, for instance. They're exempt from federal tax and usually from state tax as well, for those who live in the state that issued the bond. In general, the longer the bond term, the more interest you'll receive. So short-term bonds may not be as profitable as long-term bonds.

A benefit to investing in bonds is that your yield, or interest rate, is guaranteed. In return for that safety, you receive a relatively low rate of return. Even though bonds are considered conservative investment options because they don't offer growth potential (like stocks do), they do have some risks. Rising interest rates cause the value of a bond to decrease. That's because new bonds, issued at a higher interest rate, make the older bonds with lower rates of return less valuable. Inflation can also cause a bond's yield to become less attractive. There's the risk of prepayment, or that the issuer will pay off the bond early. There's also the risk that a bond issuer may become less credit worthy or even default on repayment of the contract altogether. Agencies do research on companies who issue bonds and offer a rating system based on their safety. For additional information on bond ratings, visit standardandpoors.com.

Some of the safest investments today are treasury bonds, which are backed by the full faith of the federal government. Treasuries, as they're called, come in various forms. Treasury bills, or T-bills, are short-term securities that can mature in as little as a few days. Treasury notes can take as long as ten years to mature. There are also savings bonds called TIPS that pay interest rates tied to inflation. If the inflation rate increases, so do the yields on those types of bonds.

MORE ABOUT TIPS

Treasury Inflation-Protected Securities (TIPS) have been offered by the federal government since 1997. They protect you against the detrimental effects of inflation. They're issued in 5, 10, and 20-year terms with fixed interest payments that are paid twice a year. The principal value is adjusted by changes in the Consumer Price Index (CPI). Therefore, the interest payments rise as inflation causes the value of the underlying security to increase or they fall when deflation occurs. However, if the security decreases in value, you're protected because when TIPS mature, you receive the adjusted principal or the original principal amount, whichever is greater. Income from TIPS is tax-exempt from state and local income taxes, just like other treasuries.

You can buy treasuries for your nonretirement portfolio through a full service broker, specialized bond broker, or directly online at savingsbonds.gov. However, you generally can't buy individual treasuries for an IRA. That's because you can't create an account in the name of an IRA—you would need the assistance of your IRA custodian to purchase treasuries directly for you. But there are plenty of bond funds that you can purchase for an IRA. And just like with stocks, workplace retirement plans may only offer bond investments through mutual funds.

Mutual Funds

Mutual funds are investment vehicles that bundle combinations of investments in stocks, bonds, assets, and other securities into packages that are very convenient for investors. Those investments would be complicated for a typical investor to manage on their own. Mutual funds allow people without financial experience to easily invest small or large amounts of money—that's why they're common investments for all types of retirement accounts. Workplace plans will usually have a menu of various categories of mutual funds for you to choose from. You can buy mutual funds though traditional or online brokerages, directly from the fund company, or even from banks. (If you purchase mutual fund shares through a bank, remember that your investment is not the same as an FDIC-insured bank account.)

Most mutual funds can be categorized as stock funds, bond funds, or money market funds. Stock mutual funds have the greatest potential risk as well as the greatest potential reward, but not all stock funds are the same. Even within the stock fund category there is a range of risk. For example, aggressive growth funds invest in stocks that have the greatest potential risk and return. And income funds focus on stocks that pay out regular dividends.

Bond mutual funds will also have a range of risk, but are generally more conservative than stock funds. The safest bond funds invest in bonds issued by the federal government, and the riskiest usually hold poorly rated, junk bonds. Money market funds have the least amount of associated risk because they're limited to holding specific high quality, short term investments.

There are also many hybrid mutual fund categories:

- **Balanced funds** combine investments in stocks, bonds, and other securities for a moderate risk offering.

- **Target-date or life-cycle funds** are a popular type of fund that invests with a certain retirement date in mind for its investors. For instance, a 2020 target-date fund manages its portfolio with the idea that the fund owner will need to retire starting in the year 2020. Fund managers rebalance a target-date fund's asset allocation in an attempt to create results and risk levels that are suitable for an investor's age and investment objectives. Managers move money from higher risk investments such as stocks to moderate and then low-risk investments as the intended retirement deadline approaches. Target-date funds have been criticized as being generic solutions for sophisticated investors who might want more customized investments. However, for many investors, target-date funds are the best way to get good asset allocation that's automatic and effortless (we'll cover asset allocation soon). I have a target-date fund in my retirement portfolio right now.

- **Index funds** try to mimic the return of various market indices such as the S&P 500 or the Dow Jones Industrial Average (DJIA). A stock market index is a group of actively traded stocks chosen for certain characteristics such as their size or market sector.

- **Small-cap, mid-cap, and large-cap funds** invest in stocks based on the size of the company. Cap is short for market capitalization and is a measure of a company's size based on its number of outstanding stock shares. Large caps are generally the oldest and most established companies.

- **International funds** invest solely in foreign companies.

- **Sector funds** invest in various financial instruments such as stocks and bonds within a particular industry such as biotechnology or consumer goods.

- **Green or socially responsible funds** only make investments related to companies that have good environmental or labor practices.

The Cost of Mutual Funds

The downside to mutual funds is that they're expensive to operate. Investors have to pay a host of fees and commissions regardless of a fund's performance. That's the case whether you own mutual funds inside of or outside of a retirement account. "Load" is another word for a sales commission that gets added on to the price of a fund. If loads are charged when you invest, it's called a front-end load. Fees are taken out before your funds are purchased, which actually reduces the amount you invest. A back-end load is charged when you sell your shares. There are some no-load funds that can be purchased directly from the fund family. However, they'll probably still charge some fees to cover the costs of management and operation. Vanguard (vanguard.com) and Schwab (schwab.com) are both companies that sell no-load mutual funds.

Many investors don't even realize that they're paying fees as high as 6 percent in some cases for mutual fund investments because they're not itemized on a statement as an obvious "charge." Fees are deducted before your money is invested or are simply taken from your account balance. That obviously puts a serious dent in your investment return. For a workplace plan, you may not have a say in the matter. You may have ten mutual funds on your retirement plan menu at work that all charge high fees, with no other choices. However, if you choose funds for your IRA or regular brokerage account, do your homework and compare the bottom-line fees. Take a look at a fund's prospectus or research it online to find out what it costs to own it. The Securities and Exchange Commission (SEC) requires full disclosure of all fees to help consumers make informed decisions.

Exchange Traded Funds (ETFs)

Exchange Traded Funds are innovative investment funds that have been around since the early 1990s. One of the reasons for their growing popularity is that they combine the flexibility of investing in individual stocks with the diversity of investing in mutual funds. When you invest in an ETF you get exposure to a basket of securities, just like with mutual funds. There are hundreds of ETFs, each created to address investment choices for various industry sectors, geographic regions, countries, company sizes, real estate, or broad market indices, for example. There are target-date ETFs that allow you to choose a fund that matches the year when you plan to access the money. They can be bought and sold just like shares of stock of publicly held companies.

One major advantage of investing in ETFs is their low cost. The percentage of fund assets that are spent to operate the fund is very low when compared to many mutual funds. ETFs have no investment minimums or extra sales charges. However, you do pay a customary brokerage fee for placing a buy or sell order, just like you would to buy a stock. For more information about investing in ETFs, visit Web sites such as ishares.com and powershares.com.

Should You Invest in ETFs or Mutual Funds?

If you're going to invest by dollar-cost averaging (that's contributing small amounts of money on a consistent basis—I'll talk more about that later in this chapter), a low-expense mutual fund may be a better choice for you than an ETF. That's because each time you purchase shares of an ETF you have to pay a customary brokerage commission, which could range anywhere from $8 to $30—even at an online discount brokerage. However, if you invest larger amounts of money on a not-so-regular basis, you'll probably have lower transaction costs buying an ETF instead of a mutual fund. But be sure to do your own research on the expenses associated with any investment.

The big buzz surrounding ETFs is that they're more tax efficient than mutual funds. Here's why in a nutshell: When a mutual fund manager buys and sells investments in their fund, it can result in a capital gain, which is profit that's taxable. The tax liability gets passed along to the mutual fund shareholders, but the good news is that's only a problem when you own mutual funds in a taxable account. When you own mutual funds in a retirement account, taxes are either deferred or eliminated, which we'll cover in detail in the next chapter.

Here's a quick and dirty tip: Use the Fund Analyzer at finra.org, the Web site of the Financial Industry Regulatory Authority, to compare the effect that various fund fees will have on over 18,000 products that include mutual funds and ETFs.

DIVERSIFICATION

Earlier in this chapter we were talking about investing and risk; no discussion about risk is complete without including the concept of diversification. Diversification is a way to manage risk by spreading it out among multiple investments in your portfolio. For example, it could mean holding multiple stocks instead of just one. That way, if one stock is a loser, you have other winners to count on. Diversification is just like the classic saying: DON'T PUT ALL YOUR EGGS IN ONE BASKET. If you have a dozen eggs in the same basket, one wrong move could smash all of them. Diversification requires you to put one egg in each of twelve baskets. That way if one or two baskets get dropped, you only lose a couple of eggs instead of all twelve. When you diversify, you attempt to dilute potential risk by allowing profitable investments to neutralize unprofitable ones. When you have a variety of investments, it's not likely that they all could go bust at the same time. But if you have all your money in one security, for instance, it could drop in value at the exact time you're counting on it to fund your child's education or your own retirement.

Asset Allocation

Asset allocation is an important way to achieve diversification. It's mixing different asset classes or categories into your portfolio to help reduce risk. Instead of owning just stocks, for example, you would spread your investment dollars over more classes of assets such as:

1. **Cash and cash equivalents:** checking, savings, money market deposit accounts, CDs, money market mutual funds

Here's a quick and dirty tip: If you invest in a workplace retirement plan, never own more than 10 percent of your total account value in your company stock.

2. **Bonds and bond funds:** fixed-income investments with different maturities from private and public sources and various countries
3. **Stock and stock funds:** equity investments in companies of different sizes in various industry sectors and countries

Cash, bonds, and stocks are the three major asset classes, but there are others such as real estate and commodities—like gold, wheat, or oil, for example. Investing in combinations of asset classes that aren't related to each other will help you improve your returns and limit your losses because each class has its own economic cycle, level of volatility, and risk. That's because they respond to financial conditions differently. For example, an economic event that causes a decrease in bond income may trigger an increase in the value of your stocks. If your portfolio includes the right blend of asset classes you're less exposed to risk and therefore more likely to get higher total returns.

There's no precise formula that tells you exactly what your asset allocation should be. You might decide that the right mix of assets for your desired level of risk is 60 percent stocks, 30 percent bonds, and 10 percent real estate, for example. However, your portfolio should be rebalanced on a regular basis depending on changing market conditions and your investment time horizon, at least annually. Why? Consider this: If your portfolio consists of 60 percent stocks, 30 percent bonds, and 10 percent real estate when the market is up, when the market goes down you might be left with 50 percent stocks, 40 percent bonds, and 10 percent real estate. The market's decline is likely to reduce the value of some of your stocks. So you'll need to rebalance to get back to your desired allocation of 60/30/10. You accomplish that by buying more stock and selling some bonds. That way when the market goes back up, you're set to make big earnings on your stock holdings. So remember that the idea isn't to buy and hold—but to buy and rebalance! That keeps your investment funds growing without taking unreasonable risks.

Since many individuals don't have the expertise to invest in different types of assets, mutual funds and ETFs have come to the rescue! They give you inexpensive diversification whether you choose to invest in small or large amounts of shares. As I mentioned, mutual fund and ETF life-cycle or target-date funds automatically rebalance based on the fund's stated objective. Investing in a target-date fund is an easy way to keep your money protected and to meet your long-term financial goals. Learn more about target-date funds from companies like Fidelity (fidelity.com), T. Rowe Price (troweprice.com), and iShares (ishares.com).

Although diversification and asset allocation are excellent strategies to reduce risk, it's important to understand that they can't guarantee that you won't lose money in a declining market. In 2008, many investors with broad diversification saw almost all asset classes plunge in value. Few investors escaped losses during that historic bear market.

DOLLAR-COST AVERAGING

One of the most convenient and effective strategies to build long-term wealth is to invest by dollar-cost averaging (DCA). That means investing a fixed amount of money on a consistent basis over an extended period of time. If you have a workplace retirement plan where you invest 5 percent from each weekly paycheck, for example, that's exactly what you're doing. DCA allows you to build

---

Here's a quick and dirty tip: As a very rough guideline, subtract your age from 100 and use that number as the percentage of stock to have in your portfolio. For example, if you're forty, you might consider holding 60 percent of your portfolio in stocks. The remaining 40 percent would be in various other asset classes such as bonds, real estate, and cash.

wealth regardless of what the financial markets are doing. Here's an example:

> Sally earns $1,000 a week as an accounting manager. She's been participating in her workplace retirement account since the first day she was eligible and contributes 5 percent of her pay, or $50 a week. She invests her money in a stock mutual fund. Last week her fund's price was $25 per share, therefore she was able to purchase two shares with her $50 investment. However, this week her fund's price dropped to $20 per share. That means that her $50 investment buys two and a half shares ($50 investment ÷ $20 price per share = 2.5 shares) this week.

With DCA, a temporary dip in the value of Sally's investment allowed her to buy more shares for her money. Here's an example of what happens if the stock market rallies the following week and pushes the price of her fund up:

> Let's say the price of Sally's fund shot up from $20 per share to $30 per share. Remember that she has $50 to invest each week, so her money will only buy her 1.67 shares this week ($50 investment ÷ $30 price per share = 1.67 shares).

With DCA, you invest the same amount of money in the same investment over and over. So when the investment share price is up, you get fewer shares for your money; when the price is down, you get more shares for your money. The same investment buys you different quantities of shares each time you invest, which gives you an average cost per share over time. This strategy saves you the effort of closely watching market movements and trying to time your investments to buy shares only when prices are low. It's tempting to want to buy investments more aggressively when prices are moving up or to sell them when prices are dropping, but for the vast majority of investors it's best to stick to a consistent DCA strategy in all markets.

Dollar-cost averaging can be done with any type of investment, but it works best with low-fee mutual funds, which are perfect for investors who don't have a large amount to invest. They're an inexpensive way to make smaller investments on a regular basis because you don't have to pay a flat brokerage commission, like you do when purchasing stocks for example. DCA can be less risky than investing a large amount of money all at once. Dollar-cost averaging will help you get better returns as the market slowly increases in value over your investment horizon. It ensures that your average cost per share represents both the highs and the lows that an investment experiences over time. Bull markets (those that trend up) and bear markets (those that trend down) can last for months or years. But DCA works to smooth out the bumps and volatility of the market, which makes it a recommended strategy for your long-term investment goals such as retirement. It allows you to build a strong portfolio over time with minimal timing risk.

INVEST OR PAY DOWN DEBT?

Okay, so investing is an important way to grow rich. But what if you have debt to pay off? If you have extra money left over at the end of the month or you receive a cash windfall is it better to invest your spare cash or to use it to pay down debt? It's likely that you want to pay off your debt as soon as possible, but it's also true that you want to invest for the future so you'll have financial security. As with just about everything else in personal finance, the answer to the "invest or pay down debt" question depends on your situation. We've already talked about the importance of paying off your dangerous debt as soon as possible. For example, if you have overdue child support, tax bills, or legal judgments, you need to put your money toward paying off those debts as quickly as possible. I recommend that you get rid of your highest-interest, non-tax deductible debt (such as credit cards, payday, and car loans) next, before you consider putting your extra money toward investing.

Determine the Highest Return on Your Money

When you boil down the investing-versus-debt-reduction issue, the real question is which option will bring you the highest return on your money. In other words, what's more profitable: investing with the expectation that your money will grow or saving the interest expense that you have to pay on your debt? When you pay off debt early, you're actually earning a guaranteed interest rate that you'd otherwise have to pay.

The tricky part about this issue is that income taxes come into play. Taxes can make a huge difference because they make some investments (held outside of retirement accounts) less profitable but they also make some debts (like mortgages, HELOCs, and student loans for eligible taxpayers) less costly. To correctly evaluate whether you should pay down a debt early instead of choosing to invest the money, you need know the after-tax interest rate for both options. That shows you what a debt costs you after taxes or what an investment will earn for you after taxes. Taking taxes into consideration is so important because it allows you to make an "apples to apples" comparison using the real numbers. We'll talk more about taxes in chapter 10, but follow me through this scenario:

Cindy has $150 left over in her budget each month after she invests in her retirement plan at work and pays all her monthly expenses. She's wondering whether to invest the $150 or to send the money to her mortgage as an extra principal payment each month. Cindy has an interest-only mortgage of $200,000 with a 5 percent annual interest rate. That means she pays a total of $10,000 per year in interest ($200,000×0.05=$10,000). But since she claims the home mortgage interest tax deduction, her mortgage actually costs her less than $10,000 a year. The deduction allows Cindy to subtract $10,000 from her taxable earnings each year. And as you probably know, less taxable income means less tax to pay.

The amount Cindy will save in taxes by claiming the home mortgage interest deduction depends on her income tax rate. Her income puts her in the 25% tax bracket. Twenty-five percent of her $10,000 tax deduction equals $2,500*. So, reducing her taxable income by $10,000 allows her to save $2,500 in taxes. And if

---

* *This example uses a flat tax calculation of 25 percent for illustrative purposes. In chapter 10, we'll discuss how the marginal federal tax rate is actually calculated.*

she doesn't owe any taxes, she'll receive that money as a tax refund.

When the tax deduction is taken into account, you can see that the real annual cost of the interest on Cindy's mortgage isn't $10,000—it's reduced by her tax savings of $2,500. So the interest she pays on her mortgage effectively costs her just $7,500 per year. If you divide $7,500 by her mortgage balance of $200,000, you get her after-tax annual interest rate, which is just 3.75 percent—not too bad!

So if Cindy uses her spare cash to pay off her mortgage early, that would give her a guaranteed 3.75 percent annual return. The question is whether she can find a better way to use the money that would yield a higher after-tax return. There are so many different ways she could invest, but let's say she found a tax-free municipal bond fund with a ten-year historical performance that would earn 5 percent, including fund fees. Since earning a 5 percent return is higher than getting a 3.75 percent savings from paying down her mortgage, choosing to invest is the more profitable option for Cindy. But remember that taking the investment route is speculative and involves a level of risk.

Pros and Cons of Paying Off Debt Versus Investing

Whether you should use your excess money to pay down debt or to invest in your future is a hotly debated topic in personal finance. My recommendation is to invest your extra money whenever the after-tax earnings are expected to be higher than the after-tax interest rate on your debt. However, the best solution for you should depend on your tolerance for risk and your long-term financial goals. If you still feel conflicted about the issue, one solution is to do both. You could send half your spare cash to pay down low-interest debt and the other half to build wealth in a higher-yielding investment.

PROTECT YOURSELF

Smart investors use a method of choosing investments that includes good ol' common sense. If something sounds too good to be true, well, you know the rest. I mentioned that investing always involves some amount of risk, but that shouldn't be confused with gambling. Many times investors lose money because they invest in something that they don't fully understand. The Bernie Madoff Ponzi scheme comes to mind. Madoff duped thousands of investors into a fraudulent and long-running scam that cost them tens of billions of dollars. Before his incarceration, he admitted to simply moving money between accounts to create an impression of trading and then sending false trade statements to clients. A Ponzi scheme is an operation that promises a consistent, high return to investors. The attractive returns are paid to investors out of money received from new investors. That house of cards holds up only as long as there's a steady stream of new investors injecting money into the operation. Ponzis eventually collapse under their own weight when they get so big that the inflow of new money can't cover all the promised payouts.

Here are some danger signs to watch out for that may be indications of a Ponzi scheme:

1. **The promise of an unusually high or consistent return on investment.** This is almost impossible to achieve from legitimate investments because their value fluctuates over time.

2. **One central person who has a top secret investing formula.** Any investment that relies on the expertise of one person should raise your suspicion.

3. **A lack of transparency about underlying investments.** There's no substitute for detailed financial information. Protect yourself by requesting statements that have been audited by a reputable accounting firm.

4. **An urgency to recruit new investors.** High-pressure sales tactics may be used over the phone or in person. Be very wary of unsolicited investment offers you may find in a fax, e-mail, or Internet posting.

5. **Persuasion to invest targeted toward religious or affinity groups.** Con men are so named because they're out to gain your

Here's a quick and dirty tip: Do independent research before investing your money to make sure you understand a company's business model, products or services, and legitimacy. Being an educated investor is your best defense against falling prey to fraud.

confidence. They try to deceive people who don't have much financial knowledge or won't ask many questions.

Now that we've covered the key concepts about creating wealth, let's get into the details about how to really make it happen using the different types of retirement accounts.

7

Planning for Retirement

> Retirement at sixty-five is ridiculous. When I was sixty-five I still had pimples.
>
> —GEORGE BURNS, comedian

Now that we've talked about the different types of investments and important investment concepts, you're ready to use that information when thinking about your retirement accounts. The various types of retirement accounts can seem confusing at first, but I promise that getting to know them will be worth your time. They offer you an extra layer of protection because the government offers tax-deferred or tax-free growth on the money you put into qualified retirement accounts. That means you save money on taxes and have more money for retirement! When you make money on investments held outside of a retirement account you generally have to pay tax on the income each year. But that's not the case with investments held inside of retirement accounts. Whether you're a stay-at-home mom, an employee, or self-employed, you have the ability to use tax-favored retirement accounts to your advantage. There are Individual Retirement Arrangements (IRAs), various qualified workplace plans, and in some cases nonqualified workplace plans that can help you build a nest egg as quickly as possible.

As a side note: Throughout this book I'll give you the most current information that's available at the time of writing. The IRS reevaluates each year to see if regulations should be changed. So always refer to irs.gov for the most up-to-date information.

RETIREMENT ACCOUNTS FOR INDIVIDUALS

First, let's talk about the funding vehicle that's a cornerstone to retirement—the IRA, or Individual Retirement Arrangement. It's a personal savings plan that gives the vast majority of U.S. taxpayers the ability to save considerable taxes on the growth of their retirement nest egg. It's available to anyone, regardless of age, who receives taxable compensation during the year. IRAs can only be owned by individuals; they can't be owned jointly, so you and your partner or spouse cannot own one together. IRAs can be set up at a variety of institutions such as banks, mutual funds, traditional brokerages, or online brokerages. The funds in an IRA can be put in many types of investments and bank accounts that we've discussed, such as stocks, bonds, mutual funds, ETFs, or CDs.

Traditional and Roth Accounts

There are two main types of IRAs: traditional and Roth accounts. Roth IRAs get their name from the late Senator William Roth of Delaware, who sponsored their legislation. Traditional and Roth IRAs are alike in many ways, but a defining difference between the two is how they're taxed. With a traditional IRA you generally don't pay taxes on the money you earn and put into the account. You pay taxes on that money and all future earnings after you reach the official retirement age of fifty-nine and a half and begin to take qualified distributions from the account. That gives you an immediate tax break because you defer paying taxes on the money you earn and contribute to a traditional IRA until some time in the future. If you contribute money to a traditional IRA that was already taxed (such as employment income that had payroll taxes deducted) you get to take a tax deduction for the amount on your income tax return. However, the deduction you can take depends on your income and whether you or a spouse were also covered by a workplace retirement plan during the tax year.

Contributions to a Roth IRA are just the opposite because they're made with posttax dollars. You pay tax on money you earn before you contribute it to a Roth, but you don't pay any more tax on that money or on earnings when you withdraw it in the future. Once you reach fifty-nine and a half and decide to start taking qualified distributions from a Roth, your retirement gift will be no taxes to pay on that nest egg. You get a huge tax benefit with a Roth because your entire account grows completely tax-free!

Who's Eligible to Contribute to an IRA?

Traditional IRAs are available to anyone who's received taxable income and is younger than age seventy and a half by the end of the tax year. Roth IRAs are also available to anyone—no matter your age—who's received taxable income during the year, but you must make less than a certain amount of income (see below). For a Roth, you don't have to be younger than age seventy and a half to make a contribution—you can continue to fund it every year for the rest of your life, if you wish. You can make contributions to either type of IRA even if you have another retirement plan at work. However, depending on your income level, some or all of your contributions may not be tax deductible if you or your spouse also has an employer-sponsored retirement plan in addition to an IRA.

As I just mentioned, to be eligible to contribute to a Roth, there are limits on how much you can earn:

- For those filing taxes as Single, Head of Household, or Married Filing Separately (if you did not live with your spouse during the year): When your modified adjusted gross income (MAGI) is $120,000 or more you cannot make a Roth IRA contribution.

- For those filing taxes as Married Filing Jointly or Qualifying Widow(er): When MAGI is $177,000 or more you cannot make a Roth IRA contribution.

- For those filing taxes as Married Filing Separately (if you did live with your spouse during the year): When MAGI is $10,000 or more you cannot make a Roth contribution.

Here's a quick and dirty tip: If you expect a refund at tax time, have it paid directly to your IRA. To do that, submit Form 8888, which is available on the IRS Web site at irs.gov.

These are the 2010 income limits and it's likely that the IRS will adjust them up slightly in future years. Check the Cost-of-Living Increases link at irs.gov/retirement for updated information.

How Much Can You Contribute to an IRA?

There are not only restrictions on who can contribute to an IRA, there are also restrictions on how much you can contribute. The maximum amount you can contribute to a traditional or Roth IRA is your total taxable compensation or $5,000 for 2010, whichever is smaller. For example, if you're a student who made $3,000 in 2010, you can only contribute a maximum of $3,000 to your IRA. If you're an account executive who made $45,000 in 2010, you can only contribute $5,000. Taxable income for IRA purposes includes wages, salaries, bonuses, commissions, tips, net self-employment income, and alimony. Compensation that isn't counted for IRA purposes includes income from pensions, annuities, dividends, interest, and profit from rental property, for example. You can own more than one traditional or Roth IRA, but total contributions to all your IRAs may not exceed your annual contribution limit. If you're age fifty or older, catch-up provisions allow you to save an additional $1,000 (for a total of $6,000 for 2010) to your traditional or Roth IRA(s). There is no minimum or required annual IRA contribution. If you choose to contribute, you can do so at any time during the year up until taxes are due in April following the tax year, not including any extensions of time to file. So for 2011 contributions, you have until April 15 of 2012 to fund your IRA(s), even if you file for a tax deadline extension.

For Roth IRAs, there are reduced contribution limits as follows:

- For those filing taxes as Single, Head of Household, or Married Filing Separately (if you did not live with your spouse during the year): When your modified adjusted gross income (MAGI) is $105,000 up to $120,000, your contribution limit is phased out (reduced).

- For those filing taxes as Married Filing Jointly or Qualifying Widow(er): When MAGI is $167,000 up to $177,000, your contribution limit is phased out.
- For those filing taxes as Married Filing Separately (if you did live with your spouse during the year): When MAGI is zero to $10,000, your contribution limit is phased out.

The reduced contribution limits are figured using a somewhat complicated IRS worksheet that's in Publication 590. They give an example of a forty-five-year-old single taxpayer with MAGI of $106,000. The steps and calculations in the worksheet show that her maximum IRA contribution would be $4,670.

WHAT'S A SPOUSAL IRA?

There's a special provision that allows both spouses to have traditional or Roth IRAs, even if one doesn't work or has taxable income that's less than the allowable contribution limit. If you're married and file a joint tax return, the total combined contributions that can be made for the year to your IRA and to your spouse's IRA can be as much as $10,000 (or $11,000 if one of you is age fifty or older or $12,000 if both of you are age fifty or older). The only limitation is that as a couple you must have at least $10,000 of taxable income. Here's an example:

Reggie and Stephanie are married and are both fifty-five years old. Reggie works full-time and earned $80,000, while Stephanie earned $4,000 working part-time. Even though Stephanie earned less than $5,000, if she and Reggie file a joint return, they can contribute $6,000 to her IRA and $6,000 to his IRA. They each get to contribute $5,000 plus an additional $1,000 because they're over age fifty. If they were to file taxes separately, Stephanie would only be able to contribute $4,000—the amount of her taxable income.

Here's a quick and dirty tip: If your income increases to the point that you aren't eligible to contribute to a Roth IRA anymore, you can let the Roth account sit idle and contribute to a traditional IRA instead.

Should You Convert to a Roth IRA?

Many people would love to take advantage of tax-free growth in a Roth IRA but they make too much money to be eligible. Even if you don't qualify, it's still possible to convert a traditional IRA into a Roth. Starting on January 1 of 2010, anyone can make a Roth conversion, regardless of income, which is great news for high earners. In the past, you had to earn less than $100,000 in the year that you wanted to do a Roth conversion to be eligible—which put the Roth conversion out of reach for many. The income limits to contribute (see above) still apply, so you won't be able to make additional contributions to your Roth if you're a high earner, but you'll still have your converted retirement money growing tax-free as long as you keep it in the account.

The downside of doing a Roth conversion is that you have to pay tax on any funds that weren't already taxed. But you don't have to convert all the money in a traditional IRA—you can convert just a portion of it if you wish.

Whether doing a Roth conversion is best for you can be a tricky issue because there are lots of variables to consider. If you decide to do a conversion, contact the custodian of your IRA and let them know your plan. But it's a good idea to speak with an accountant or a financial advisor to review your situation first. Here are four questions to help you think over some of the major issues involved in doing a Roth conversion:

1. Do you think U.S. income tax rates will be higher in the future, when you'll need your IRA money? If so, paying a lower tax rate now for a Roth conversion is a better option than paying a higher tax rate on traditional IRA funds later on.

Here's a quick and dirty tip: At dinkytown.com, the Roth IRA Conversion Calculator will show you what advantage, if any, doing a conversion will give you. Use their Roth vs. Traditional IRA Calculator to help understand which type of account may be right for you.

2. Do you think your personal income tax bracket will be higher when you retire than it is now? That's usually the case for young workers who are just beginning their careers. Again, paying less tax sooner, rather than more tax later (on an amount that has potentially grown much larger over time), is better.

3. Can you pay the tax liability for converted funds from sources other than your IRA? Taking money out of an IRA to pay for conversion taxes is a bad idea because it reduces your account value and triggers an early withdrawal penalty (see the next section).

4. Did your traditional IRA take a beating in the last couple of years? If it hasn't fully recovered, having a lower account value means you'll pay less conversion taxes than if the account value was higher. That's a way to make lemonade out of financial lemons! For example, if your traditional IRA was worth $50,000 at its peak and now is worth $35,000, you only pay Roth conversion taxes on the current value of $35,000.

How to Get Money Out of an IRA

What happens when you need to get money out of an IRA? The reason you receive tax advantages from the government for a retirement account is so you'll keep the money saved until you reach retirement age. Withdrawing money from an IRA prior to age fifty-nine and a half can trigger a 10 percent tax penalty; however, there are exceptions. You may not have to pay the 10 percent penalty if you use the money to pay for "qualified" priorities such as an IRS tax levy, medical expenses, educational expenses, a first home, or if you're disabled, the beneficiary of an IRA, receive distributions in the form of an annuity, or if you roll over funds to another qualified retirement plan in a timely manner.

For a traditional IRA, an early withdrawal will usually be subject to ordinary income tax in addition to the 10 percent penalty that I just mentioned. Mandatory distributions for traditional IRAs begin on April 1 after you reach age seventy and a half, or you'll pay steep excise taxes of 50 percent on what remains in the account. That's the government's way of making sure that you pay taxes on those funds (remember that you make pre-tax contributions to a traditional IRA).

For a Roth IRA, an early withdrawal may or may not be taxable. You can withdraw your contributions without penalty (remember that you make post-tax contributions to a Roth IRA). However, an early withdrawal of the earnings on your contributions prior to age fifty-nine and a half is subject to ordinary income tax in addition to the 10 percent penalty. The penalty is waived if the withdrawal is for a qualified purpose or expense, just like for a traditional IRA. Once you reach retirement age you can take distributions without penalty, as long as the account has been in place for five years. There's no mandatory distribution age for Roth IRAs.

Here's a table to help you distinguish between the major features of traditional and Roth IRAs*:

FEATURE	TRADITIONAL IRA	ROTH IRA
Annual maximum contribution	$5,000 for 2010 or $6,000 if age 50 or older by end of year	$5,000 for 2010 or $6,000 if age 50 or older by end of year
Income limits	No income limitation	$177,000 for 2010: Married filing jointly $120,000 for 2010: Single, Head of household, or Married filing separately

* As mentioned earlier, the IRS may adjust future contribution limits for IRAs. See the Cost-of-Living Increases link at irs.gov/retirement for the most up-to-date information.

FEATURE	TRADITIONAL IRA	ROTH IRA
Age you can make contributions	Younger than age 70½ by the end of year	Any age
Taxation of contributions	Not taxed, contributions made with pretax dollars	Taxed, contributions made with after-tax dollars
Deduct contributions from your taxable income	Amount depends on your income, filing status, and other retirement account coverage	No deductions allowed
Requirement to take distributions	Must begin taking minimum distributions by April 1 after you reach age 70½	No required distributions at any age
Taxation of withdrawals after age 59½	Taxed as ordinary income	Not taxed if account was held for at least 5 years

Self-Directed IRAs

Earlier in this section I mentioned that the funds in an IRA can be put in a variety of investments and bank accounts such stocks, bonds, mutual funds, or CDs. There's also a way to put your retirement money in more nontraditional investments. If you're interested in very active management of your IRA, you can create a self-directed IRA; for business owners there are other options, such as the self-directed 401(k). Self-directed retirement accounts allow you to make extremely diversified and sophisticated investments within your IRA, such as domestic and foreign real estate, mortgages, tax liens, businesses, and precious metals. Many people who like real estate investments such as vacant land, houses, condos, commercial properties, foreclosures, and rental properties can benefit from owning them inside a self-directed IRA. The only two types of investments that you can't purchase in a self-directed retirement account are life insurance contracts and collectibles, such as antiques, art, and cars.

Self-directed IRAs have the same basic rules as regular IRAs. However, self-directed retirement accounts also have additional restrictions, especially when it comes to using IRA funds to buy real estate. So if you like the idea of purchasing real estate with your IRA money, you'll need to brush up on the various account restrictions to protect yourself. The limitations were established to prevent assets in self-directed accounts from benefiting the account owner in any way until he or she reaches retirement age. You see, according to the IRS, the funds in a self-directed retirement account are only meant to benefit the account—not the account owner who's investing them. If you use money or assets held in your self-directed IRA for personal benefit before the law allows, you're engaging in what's called a "self-dealing" transaction. That violates the rules and puts the tax-deferred status of an account in jeopardy. That could mean having to face a massive tax bill. Consider this example:

You're forty years old and decide to use $50,000 in your self-directed IRA to pay cash for some vacant land on a small lake. You want to purchase the lot now, while it's still for sale at an affordable price. You intend to take ownership of the property and build a cozy cabin on it once you retire. Until then, you plan on going to the lot on summer weekends to launch your canoe and do some fishing. Sounds innocent enough, right? Well, that plan would actually be a bad idea. Because you purchased the land with IRA funds, you'd be violating the tax law by deriving any personal benefit from the property before retirement age. If the IRS were to wise up to your personal use of the land, the entire value of the property could be considered a nonqualified IRA distribution. That means the full value of the property would be subject to income tax plus an early withdrawal penalty since you're younger than age fifty nine and a half.

Here's another scenario:

You want to buy a beach house with your self-directed IRA and rent it out for income until you can use it as a second home when you retire. That's completely legit as long as you follow the rules.

The major restriction for your beach house is that until you retire, you can't use it as a vacation property, even for a weekend. Nor can you rent it out to certain close relatives. You aren't even allowed to pay yourself the profits generated by an IRA's rental property—those must go back into the retirement account.

So, you can see that investors must be extremely careful about how they use the funds and assets held in a self-directed retirement account. Getting started with one is pretty easy. You can set it up with new money or transfer funds from an existing IRA. Custodial firms, insurance companies, and banks can open up the account and act as your trustee and oversee the transactions. They handle the disbursement of funds or collection of profits for the IRA, but they might not give you investment advice or even handle real estate transactions. For that reason, it's best to find an administrator with specialized real estate experience. Due to the complex regulations for self-directed accounts, you should seek the guidance of a legal professional for further education before setting one up.

If you haven't done so already, I hope all these great features of traditional and Roth IRAs will prompt to you open one and start funding it right away. If you're an employee, some companies may offer a payroll deduction IRA. This allows you to authorize your employer to deduct and deposit your contribution from your paycheck directly to your IRA before you ever see the money or have payroll taxes deducted from it.

RETIREMENT ACCOUNTS FOR EMPLOYEES

IRAs are investment vehicles that you open up and contribute to on your own. But many lucky people also have the option to invest in a plan at work that's set up by their employer. I'll discuss the variety of common employer-sponsored qualified retirement plans in this section. One of the great features of workplace plans is that they're portable, which means you can take them with you when you leave a job. Many qualified workplace retirement plans come in traditional as well as Roth classifications.

There are two main types of qualified retirement programs

found in the workplace: defined benefit plans and defined contri-bution plans. A defined benefit plan is sponsored, funded, and completely managed by an employer. They promise a specific, defined benefit that a worker will receive at retirement, like $1,000 per month until their date of death. The benefit is calculated using factors such as age, length of employment, and earnings history to determine a set retirement payout. These benefit plans include the typical, old-fashioned pension, where an employee doesn't have to pick funds or manage their money in any way. Defined benefit programs have become rare in the workplace because they're expensive to operate and are somewhat risky for employers.

The other type of workplace retirement plan, the defined contribution plan, is established by the employer but requires that the employee manage it. An amount to contribute from each paycheck is established by the employee, but the eventual retirement benefit that the worker will receive is unknown. The ultimate benefit depends on the amount that's invested and the performance of the funds over the years. Defined contribution plans allow a worker to choose the types of investment vehicles they prefer, and therefore they carry the burden of risk. Money is deducted from paychecks before the employee receives it and is invested on a pretax basis, except where Roth options are available.

The Popular 401(k) Plan

The most popular and well-known defined contribution plan available in the workplace today is the 401(k), named after its section of the IRS code. It allows you to have an employer contribute a portion of your cash wages to the plan. A 401(k) plan generally offers participants a menu of investment choices. Total contributions to a 401(k) for 2010 are limited to $16,500, but if you're fifty years of age or older you can contribute a maximum of $22,000.

Our friend, the Roth, is also now available as a 401(k). Just like with the Roth IRA, you invest posttax money into a Roth 401(k) and it grows completely tax-free. Many employers are choosing to add the Roth option to their plan document. You can contribute to both a regular 401(k) and Roth 401(k) at the same time. Just

Here's a quick and dirty tip: Never take a loan from a workplace retirement account if you can help it. If you leave a job or are fired you usually have to repay it in full within ninety days or the loan is considered an early withdrawal, subject to a 10 percent penalty.

remember that your total contributions to both can't exceed the annual limit set by the IRS. A special feature of Roth 401(k)s is that there's no income limit placed on investors, as there is with a Roth IRA.

Distributions from both a traditional and a Roth 401(k) can begin at age fifty-nine and a half, and they must begin by age seventy and a half, otherwise penalties will apply unless the employee is still working. Early withdrawals from both types of 401(k)s are usually subject to a 10 percent penalty. However, many 401(k) plans allow for loans or limited hardship withdrawals, which mean that for specific emergency needs, the 10 percent penalty may not apply. The portion of an early withdrawal from a Roth 401(k) that's attributed to an employee's contributions is not taxed. It's best to consult with the benefits administrator at work and to be familiar with your retirement plan document.

Here's a chart to help you distinguish between the major features of traditional and Roth 401(k)s:

FEATURE	TRADITIONAL 401(K)	ROTH 401(K)
Annual maximum elective contribution	$16,500 for 2010 or $22,000 if age 50 or older by end of year	$16,500 for 2010 or $22,000 if age 50 or older by end of year
Income Limits	No limitation to participate	No limitation to participate
Taxation of contributions	Not taxed—contributions made with pretax dollars	Taxed—contributions made with after-tax dollars

FEATURE	TRADITIONAL 401(K)	ROTH 401(K)
Requirement to take distributions	Must begin taking minimum distributions by April 1 after age 70½ unless still working	Must begin taking minimum distributions by April 1 after age 70½ unless still working
Taxation of withdrawals after age 59½	Taxed as ordinary income	Not taxed if account was held for at least 5 years

403(b) Plans

Another defined contribution plan available in the workplace is the 403(b), which also gets its name from the IRS code. This plan is available for employees of certain charitable, religious, educational, and tax-exempt organizations. It's similar to a 401(k) in most aspects except that investment options are limited to mutual funds and annuities. There is a traditional as well as a Roth option for 403(b) plans.

457 Plans

The 457 plans are a third type of defined contribution workplace plan. They're for employees and independent contractors of certain tax-exempt organizations and state and local governments. The 457s are similar to 401(k) and 403(b) plans, except that there's no penalty for making early withdrawals before the age of fifty-nine and a half. Another difference is that there's no set minimum retirement age nor is there an option for participants to make Roth contributions.

WHAT IS EMPLOYER MATCHING?

If you could make a 100 percent guaranteed return on your money, would you be interested? Many people don't realize that that's what

Here's a quick and dirty tip: If you are eligible to invest in a workplace retirement plan, contribute a percentage of your earnings, rather than a flat dollar amount. As your income rises, or you qualify for bonuses, your contributions will automatically rise to the occasion!

employer matching gives you. The tax benefits of workplace retirement plans are fabulous, but when they're combined with employer matching, workplace plans are truly powerful. Many employers that offer 401(k)s and 403(b)s contribute funds to your account that match a certain percentage of your annual contributions. For example, if your employer matches 100 percent of your contributions up to 3 percent of your salary, that's a 100 percent return to you on any amount that you contribute up to the 3 percent threshold. If your salary is $30,000, and you contribute $75 a month, or $900 a year, that's a contribution of 3 percent of your salary. With 100 percent matching, your employer would also contribute $900 to your retirement account. You invest $900 and automatically get $900 from your employer—a 100 percent return on your money! That doesn't even take into account the growth your chosen investments may achieve for both your contributions and your matched money.

Here's an example of how powerful employer matching can be to your retirement savings:

> Let's say you earn $50,000 a year and decide to contribute $50 a week to your 401(k). If your employer gives you a 100 percent match on all contributions up to 3 percent of your salary, that's $1,500. So in addition to saving $2,600 ($50×52 weeks) of your own money, you receive an extra $1,500 from your employer, for a grand total of $4,100 ($2,600+$1,500) savings per year. If you consistently invested that same amount over thirty years for an average return of 6 percent, the matching would increase your total savings from $204,000 to over $326,000. Thanks to compounding interest, that's an extra $122,000 you'd have to fund your retirement lifestyle! (It's likely that your salary would increase over the span of thirty years, and that would increase your employer's match even more.)

An employer may also have a Profit Sharing Plan, which is typically coupled with a 401(k). Profit sharing is a voluntary incentive designed to reward productivity and the achievement of company goals. Those additional contributions can be subject to a vesting schedule. That means that you must stay employed for a certain period of time in order to take ownership of profit sharing funds. If you're terminated or leave prior to meeting a vesting schedule, you forfeit all or a portion of the company-provided funds. An example of a typical vesting schedule might be that after two years of service an employee is 20 percent vested, after three years they are 40 percent vested and so on. You are always 100 percent vested in contributions that you make from your wages.

SAFE HARBOR AND AUTO ENROLLMENT 401(K) PLANS

A safe harbor 401(k) plan is similar to a traditional 401(k) plan, but it generally prohibits the employer from creating a vesting schedule for company-matched funds. In other words, with a typical safe harbor plan, contributions made by your employer are immediately yours to keep. Another variation is the automatic enrollment 401(k), which allows your employer to automatically enroll you in the plan and make default salary deductions on your behalf, unless you opt out of the plan in writing.

Don't Miss the Match

If your company offers retirement savings matching and you haven't enrolled yet, what are you waiting for? One of my financial regrets is that I didn't take advantage of 401(k) savings plans earlier in my career. When I was in my twenties, I worked for a couple of companies that offered 401(k) plans with matching funds, but I didn't participate in them. Looking back, I foolishly didn't take advantage of the benefit because I thought the job might be a springboard and that I wouldn't be with the company for a long time. I also had the mistaken idea that it would be a hassle to get my money back after leaving the company. Of course, now I know how easy it is to roll over workplace retirement funds. Don't make the same mistake that I did; start contributing to an employer retirement plan the day you become eligible to participate.

You'll remember from chapter 5 that I said you should continue contributing to a company retirement plan even if you have debt to

> Here's a quick and dirty tip: If you're eligible for company matching, always invest at least the same percentage of your income that's matched by your employer. That ensures that you'll get full advantage of the benefit.

pay off. That's because once you pass on taking free money from your employer, you can't go back and ask for it later. You can try to make up for lost time by making larger contributions to your retirement accounts in the future after your debt is paid off, but it's unlikely that you'll catch up completely.

As an employee, you're fortunate to have any type of retirement plan or extra savings option at work. Retirement plans are costly for your employer to create and administer. That's why they're one of the first benefits to get eliminated when a company is struggling due to a challenging marketplace or a bad economy. So I encourage you to take advantage of every opportunity an employer offers to help you build a secure financial future!

RETIREMENT ACCOUNTS FOR THE SELF-EMPLOYED

If you're self-employed, do freelance work, or run a small business, there are some great options to create your own workplace retirement benefits. When selecting a plan, the primary factors to consider are your annual income, the amount you'd like to invest for retirement, whether you have or will have employees, your comfort level with plan administration, and whether you want the option to borrow from your retirement plan.

Keogh Plan

Let's start with Keogh plans (pronounced key-o). Keoghs got their name from congressional representative Eugene Keogh from New York who sponsored the legislation that created them. They can be set up by self-employed individuals and owners of unincorporated businesses, even if you have other employment. High contribution limits make this plan popular. Keoghs allow you to contribute up to 25 percent of your earned income to a maximum of $49,000 for 2010. If you have eligible employees you're required by law to include them in the plan. You must contribute an equal percentage of each employee's income to their account as you do to your own.

The setup for a Keogh can be somewhat complicated, but it does have flexibility. It can be a defined benefit or a defined contribution plan. With Keoghs you can invest in all types of securities. And just like with other qualified plans, you can access funds as early as age fifty-nine and a half and as late as seventy and a half without incurring penalties. However, there are no catch-up provisions for those aged fifty or older with Keoghs.

SIMPLE IRA or SIMPLE 401(k) Plan

If you own a business that has fewer than 100 employees and does not have an existing retirement plan, you are eligible to create a SIMPLE IRA or SIMPLE 401(k). SIMPLE is actually an acronym for Savings Incentive Match Plan for Employees, but it's also meant to be a simplified retirement plan with relatively low costs. It's ideal as a starter plan for smaller companies that want to minimize their administrative hassles. Employees must have earned a minimum of $5,000 in the prior year to participate in a SIMPLE plan. If you withdraw money within two years of participating in a SIMPLE IRA there's a steep 25 percent penalty instead of the usual 10 percent. This is not the case for SIMPLE 401(k)s however.

Contribution limits for SIMPLE IRA and 401(k) plans are relatively low when compared to other options for the self-employed: $11,500 for 2010. Employees over the age of fifty can make an extra catch-up contribution of up to $2,500 for 2010. With SIMPLE plans, the employer is required to match employee contributions on a dollar-for-dollar basis up to 3 percent of their annual compensation. An alternative to matching is for the employer to make nonelective contributions of 2 percent of each employee's compensation. If the nonelective option is preferred, the employer must do so for all eligible employees whether or not they contribute to the plan. Employees are always 100 percent vested in any and all employer

SIMPLE contributions. SIMPLE plans do not allow for loans. Their funds may be transferred to another SIMPLE plan or to a traditional IRA or Roth IRA, but not to another type of qualified plan.

Simplified Employee Pension (SEP)

Another retirement plan designed for the self-employed or an owner with a business of any size is the Simplified Employee Pension or SEP. It's also a simplified plan with relatively low costs that can be adopted if you don't have any other retirement plan. It's also known as a SEP-IRA because employers make contributions to IRAs set up for eligible employees. Those accounts can only be funded by the employer and the employee is always 100 percent vested in the funds. Contributions are at the discretion of the employer and do not offer a loan provision. Contribution limits may not exceed 25 percent of annual W-2 compensation or 20 percent of net self-employment income. The contribution limit for 2010 is $49,000. For those age fifty and up, there is not an additional catch-up provision as with some other plans. And SEP contributions must be made pretax because there is not a Roth option. Funds can be withdrawn as early as age fifty-nine and a half and as late as seventy and a half without incurring penalties.

Individual or Solo 401(k) Plan

The last retirement plan for the self-employed that I'll cover is the Individual 401(k). It's also known as the Solo or the Self-Employed 401(k). It's one of the newest plans to show up on the retirement scene. It may be the right choice for a business owner who works on his or her own and has no plan to hire full-time employees other than a spouse. It's similar to a regular 401(k) in that it's more costly and complex to administer than other retirement plan options. But its benefits include funding that's completely discretionary and high contribution limits. An Individual 401(k) can be set up for any type of business entity using a traditional or Roth account. As usual with Roths, contributions are made post-tax, and qualified withdrawals after the age of fifty-nine and a half are tax-free. An Individual 401(k) allows an owner to maximize their retirement contributions and have the flexibility to borrow from the plan tax-free. The 2010 contribution limit is $16,500 or $22,000 for those age fifty or older. Additionally, as the employer you can make a profit sharing contribution up to 25 percent of your compensation, not to exceed $49,000.

CAN YOU EVER TAKE EARLY WITHDRAWALS WITHOUT PENALTY?

Taking early withdrawals from most retirement accounts is usually not a good idea because, as I've mentioned, there's a steep 10 percent penalty. There are some situations where the IRS allows distributions that are not penalized, such as for first-time home buyers, higher education expenses, and medical hardships, for example. If you do need to get money out of a retirement account before the official retirement age of fifty-nine and a half, there's a little-known, legal method you can use, but it comes with restrictions and risky consequences.

The tax loophole that makes doing early withdrawals penalty-free is called a 72(t) plan. The name comes from its numbered section of the IRS tax code. 72(t)s are also known as substantially equal periodic payments, or SEPPs, and they can generally be used with retirement accounts such as IRAs, 401(k)s and 403(b)s.

Here's how 72(t) payments work: You can set up a plan to take equal monthly or annual distributions that are calculated using an accounting method that's approved by the IRS. The payment amount depends on various factors such as your retirement account balance, age, life expectancy, as well as the age and life expectancy of your account beneficiary. Once you begin taking 72(t) distributions from a retirement account, you must continue taking them for a minimum of five years or until you turn fifty-nine and a half, whichever is longer. During that time you generally can't modify the payment amount or suspend the payments. After you've completed a series of 72(t) payments, and reach the age of fifty-nine and a half, you can take retirement distributions as you see fit. However, once you reach age seventy and a half, you generally must take required minimum distributions annually from your retirement account. Another restriction of having a 72(t) plan is that you can't make additional contributions to the retirement account while you're receiving periodic payments. A violation of the rules results in a 10 percent penalty, plus interest, on all funds withdrawn prior to age fifty-nine and a half.

In challenging economic times, an increasing number of retirement account owners use 72(t) payment plans to tap their money without incurring an early withdrawal penalty. If you're facing a devastating financial hardship, draining your retirement funds prematurely may be your last resort to pay for day-to-day living expenses. Or, if you're fortunate enough to retire early, you can use a 72(t) plan to starting spending your retirement stash. If you're certain that you have enough retirement money to last as long as you'll need it, you can use 72(t) distributions to pay down or eliminate debt, pay for college tuition for family members, or to supplement your current income.

Here's an example of someone who uses a 72(t) plan to access their retirement account for needed income:

Sue was downsized from her job and offered an early retirement settlement from her company at age fifty-eight. She rolls over her 403(b) into an IRA and sets up a 72(t) plan. Even though she only has a year and a half until she reaches the official retirement age of fifty-nine and a half, she has to continue taking the 72(t) payments for five years, until she's sixty-three. At that time she can continue taking the same distribution payment or modify it to any amount that she wants.

Here's an example of someone who decides to retire early using 72(t) payments:

Alex accumulated a large nest egg well ahead of his retirement saving schedule (we should all be so lucky!). He decides to retire early and sets up a 72(t) plan for his IRA when he's fifty years old. The rule is that he must continue taking substantially equal periodic payments for five years or until he's fifty-nine and a half, whichever is longer. Since he's fifty, he can't stop taking the 72(t) distributions for nine and a half years, until his fifty-nine and a half birthday.

IMPORTANT POINTS ABOUT 72(T) PAYMENTS

When a 72(t) plan is executed properly, it can be a smart way to access your retirement funds early. But when it's set up incorrectly—with a botched pay-out schedule, for instance—it could result in expensive consequences. Therefore, it's important to set up a 72(t) payment plan only if it's absolutely necessary. Never enter into a 72(t) plan lightly or count on it to bail you out of a financial mess. The IRS rules and payment calculations for these plans are complicated, even for professionals. So if you're interested in setting up a 72(t), be sure to consult with a competent financial advisor or accountant who has specialized experience handling them.

WHAT IF NO RETIREMENT ACCOUNT OPTIONS ARE AVAILABLE TO YOU?

No matter your situation, you have options for funding your retirement. I've discussed that Social Security, or at least a portion of it, will likely be there for those who have ten years of work under their belt. And just about everyone is eligible to open and contribute to an IRA. If your employer offers a workplace retirement plan or you're self-employed and create one, you have that additional powerful savings method. If none of these options are available to you, there are always nonqualified vehicles such as conventional mutual funds, money market deposit accounts, and CDs to build the funds that will pay for your living expenses after you retire. However, you'll benefit from keeping as many of your income-producing investments (like bonds or stocks that pay dividends) as possible in a tax-advantaged account, such as a Roth IRA. Here's an example to demonstrate the potential benefit of investing within a Roth IRA:

Brad and Kim each decide to invest $50,000 in a twenty-year CD that pays 4.5 percent. They both reinvest every dividend they receive each year and are both in the 28 percent income tax bracket. Kim's CD is in her Roth IRA and Brad's is in a regular bank account.

Because Kim holds her investment in an IRA, she doesn't pay taxes on her annual interest income. Brad, on the other hand, must pay income taxes on his annual interest income because it's not in a retirement account. When their CDs reach maturity, Kim's is worth $120,585 and Brad's is worth $94,608—a difference of almost $26,000! Holding her investment in a retirement account gave Kim almost 22 percent more money.

DOING ROLLOVERS

As I mentioned, one of the benefits of retirement plans is that you have the ability to move funds without suffering any tax consequences by doing a rollover. Most people consider rollovers when they leave a job and want to take their retirement funds with them. A tax-deferred rollover occurs when you withdraw cash or assets from one eligible retirement plan and contribute it to another eligible retirement plan within sixty days. There are two ways to accomplish a retirement rollover:

1. **Indirect Rollover**: The funds are made payable to you. You deposit the money in a personal account, and then pay it to the custodian of your rollover account within sixty days.
2. **Direct Rollover**: The funds are made payable to the custodian of your retirement account.

I strongly recommend that you always do a direct rollover when you have a choice. That's because when you take a retirement distribution in your name (as with an indirect rollover) it's always subject to mandatory tax withholding of 20 percent, even if you intend to roll it over in time. Consider this example:

Kate leaves her job to relocate overseas and has $10,000 in her 401(k). She's not sure where she wants to move those funds, but she knows she wants to do a rollover. Kate elects to have the $10,000 distribution made payable to her. When she receives the check, it's only $8,000. That's because the trustee of the 401(k) is required to withhold 20 percent of all taxable distributions made to plan

> Here's a quick and dirty tip: Mandatory distributions from a Roth 401(k) after the age of seventy and a half can be avoided by rolling over funds to a Roth IRA, which doesn't require distributions at any age.

participants. So 20 percent, or $2,000, of Kate's $10,000 account balance was automatically paid to the IRS for federal income taxes, even if she plans to complete a rollover within the allowable 60 day period.

If Kate doesn't have $2,000 of her own money to replace the withheld amount, she'll only be able to rollover the $8,000 she received. If she completes the rollover within sixty days, the withheld amount will come back to her as a tax refund when she files income taxes the following year. But during that entire time Kate's $2,000 is being held by the government—instead of working for her in her retirement account!

With a direct rollover there's never any withholding taken out. It also eliminates the possibility that you could miss the sixty-day deadline for completing the rollover transaction, which would result in having to pay income tax plus an early withdrawal penalty of 10 percent on the full amount. So a direct rollover works to your advantage because it doesn't require mandatory tax withholding and leaves less room for a potential tax error to occur. If you ever have questions about doing a rollover, it's important to get advice from your retirement plan custodian. They can walk you through the process to make sure you don't break the rules and end up with a rollover that you wish you could do-over.

WHAT RETIREMENT ACCOUNT INVESTMENTS ARE RIGHT FOR YOU?

Now that you have an overview of the most common types of retirement accounts, how should you invest the money you put in them? We covered the various types of investments in the previous chapter, such as stocks, bonds, mutual funds, and ETFs. But there are different factors to consider when making your portfolio choices, such as how many years you have left before retirement and your tolerance for risk. There are various tests that have been created to help you gauge your overall like or dislike of financial risk. Try out the Investor Questionnaire at schwabmoneywise.com/resources. You'll find another good free questionnaire from Edmond Financial Group at efgi.com under the Personal tab. When I completed it, I was deemed to be "aggressive with high risk tolerance," which is one of seven risk categories that they define. They suggest a portfolio for me to achieve long-term growth using up to 75 percent stocks or stock funds. I would pretty much agree with their assessment!

If your retirement funds are in a company 401(k), your investment choices may be somewhat limited. Your portfolio decision could be as simple as deciding how to allocate your money between a few stock funds (which are more aggressive, risky options), a few bond funds (which are more conservative, less risky options), and a money market fund (the least risky option). But if you have an IRA, the mix of funds will usually be your choice. If you have more than twenty years to go before you plan to retire, you're in a great position to get a head start. Time is a critical factor in being able to amass money, due to the wonderful power of compounding interest, and as we've also discussed, time gives your portfolio the opportunity to correct itself from down markets.

When you have a long time horizon for retirement, you can afford to be more tolerant of risk. You may want as much as 80 percent or more of your portfolio in growth or aggressive growth funds when you're in your twenties and thirties. Even if it makes you a little uncomfortable, you can ride out some market losses. I'm not suggesting that you hold on to real losers, or develop an ulcer from constant worrying about every dip in the market. But not all investments can or will go up in value indefinitely. There are natural cycles to investments. They vary depending on the investment sector, the time of year, and the general state of the economy, for example. What you want to experience is a general trend of growth in your portfolio over the years.

I reviewed diversification and asset allocation in chapter 6. Spreading investment money across different types of funds and industry sectors is smart. If you're 100 percent invested in technology stocks, for example, you're open to more risk than if you were only 50 percent invested and they take a big dive. If your retirement portfolio decreases in value in a relatively short time frame such as a month or quarter, consider what else is going on in the market. Take a look at what the declining fund has done historically. Research its return on investment for the past several years. If a short-term loss seems reasonable given its long term performance, it's probably best to keep the investment.

But if any losses make you uncomfortable, consider putting larger amounts of money into safer or more conservative investments like bond funds, money market mutual funds, or CDs. Extra savings can make up for lower returns over time. Never panic and withdraw funds out of a qualified retirement plan. Early withdrawals come at a huge cost that usually isn't worth it. Even reallocating funds within your plan may cost you some profit, commissions, or taxes, depending on the situation. When you reallocate funds within a retirement plan it's not like transferring money between bank accounts. To reallocate you have to sell shares in order to buy different fund shares. If you decide to sell a fund because it's not performing well, that means you're selling at the worst possible time.

If you have online access to your workplace plan or IRA account, you can easily reallocate your investments with the click of a button. Or you can do it by completing a form with the benefits administrator at work or by contacting the brokerage firm that administers your IRA, for instance. It's important to evaluate your entire portfolio allocation at least once a year.

If you consider yourself halfway to retirement, perhaps somewhere in the range of ten to twenty years away, you'll need to take

---

Here's a quick and dirty tip: If you want to get out of a declining fund, wait for a temporary rally when the share price rises a little, before you sell or reallocate. That will help to minimize your loss.

stock of your progress. Pat yourself on the back for what you may have accomplished, but don't lose sight of your goals. You may want to consider moving some money into investments that are considered safe, such as short-term bonds or treasuries. Reallocating at least 40 percent to conservative options can be a smart idea, especially if your investment money is accumulating ahead of schedule. That's a strategy to begin preserving your wealth and reducing your exposure to market risk.

If your portfolio has lost value, give serious consideration to whether you should hold on to the losing investments. It's never a good idea to sell after prices have dropped. However, if you own investments that are fundamentally flawed you may need to cut your losses. Be realistic about the future of a company whose growth is unsustainable or an industry sector that's becoming uncompetitive, for example. Investigate any declining mutual funds you have and see what's in their portfolio. If you decide to shed any losers, be patient for a temporary rally and sell when the price isn't at rock bottom.

If you're somewhere in middle age and are just beginning your retirement planning, you'll need to put a little pressure on yourself to move the needle. Reevaluate your budget to see where you can cut expenses and start directing more of your paycheck to your retirement fund. Investing in growth funds may be necessary for you to get the kind of return that you'll need to meet your specific financial goals.

If you have less than ten years before your target retirement date, you'll need to carefully evaluate your retirement portfolio on a somewhat regular basis. Having a short time frame means you'll need conservative choices that offer safety over growth. You've worked hard to grow your savings egg, so don't let it fall out of the nest just before you're going to need it! This is the time to minimize risk by keeping a majority of your money in very safe investments like income-producing stock funds, bond funds, or CDs. If you're where you wanted to be in the financial journey to retirement, be very proud of yourself. If you're close to retirement age, but haven't saved enough, take advantage of available catch-up provisions. Those are the extra amounts you can put in retirement accounts after you're age fifty. If you have a savings shortfall, always wait to take your full Social Security benefits. That provides a higher annual income for your entire retirement. And consider what assets you have that can be sold to fund your additional needs.

Other Types of Retirement Investments

And speaking of assets, consider tangible possessions that can provide for you during retirement. If you like real estate investments, their income can be a fantastic boost to retirement savings. Once rental properties are paid off, they can provide income or be sold when the time is right. Or consider adding collectibles to build wealth for your retirement. The future value of collectibles can never be known with certainty. But if you have a passion for collecting valuable items such as rare coins, fine wine, artwork, antiques, cars, or books, for example, your hobby may be a fun way to enhance your retirement funds. Keep tabs on the appreciation of collectibles and liquidate items when you can take good profits or need to raise funds. The only danger is that you may find it difficult to part with your pride and joy!

By the time you retire, one of your largest assets may be a home that you own free and clear. If you're willing to sell it, that may provide a large lump sum of money to invest for retirement income. Whether you've paid off your property or not, you can always trade down to a less expensive home than the one you have. Or you may consider becoming a tenant and leaving the maintenance costs and hassle of home ownership to a landlord. As long as you've lived in your primary residence for two of the previous five years, you're entitled to the home sale tax exemption. That allows you to exclude $250,000 of profits from capital gains tax if you're single and $500,000 if you're married and file a joint tax return, no matter your age.

For most of us, the final destination, in financial terms, is a secure and fulfilling retirement. But we must keep our eyes on the prize. Whether the prize for you means retiring at age fifty to do full-time volunteer work, or working part-time in your own business until the day you die, it's not going to happen without a plan to make your unique vision a reality. Once you conjure up a vision of the future you'd like to have, you can work backward to the present moment to begin to create the wealth you'll need to make it happen. Start planning and building wealth as early as possible to leverage the full power of your resources for a secure financial future.

8

Buying Real Estate

> People are living longer than ever before, a phenomenon
> undoubtedly made necessary by the thirty-year mortgage.
>
> —DOUG LARSON, author

We've talked a lot about figuring out your priorities and reaching your financial goals so far in this book. For many people buying or building a home is on top of their wish list, even though it's an expensive goal. Even with declining real estate values in many markets, it's still a huge purchase that can be very confusing for most buyers. You need to know how to buy real estate wisely in order to protect yourself and pay as little as possible. In this chapter, you'll learn whether buying real estate is right for you in the first place and then, if so, how to get the best mortgage.

BUYING VERSUS RENTING

The purchase of a home can be one of life's joys as well as one of life's miseries. The first tip I'll give you about buying real estate is that it isn't for everyone. The dream of owning a home doesn't always make sense from either a financial or a lifestyle perspective. So the first question to consider is whether you should buy a home or not. For many, renting a home, condo, town house, or apartment has many more advantages than buying. That's certainly true for young people who are just starting out, but may also be true for retirees as well as certain folks of ages in between.

Pros for Renting

One of the biggest benefits of renting versus buying real estate is that it costs much less up front. For a lease, the most you usually pay is a deposit in the range of one to three times the monthly rent. For a home purchase you need to have a down payment as high as 20 percent of the purchase price, depending on your situation. When economic times are tough, many homeowners and apartment communities are willing to offer nice deals to lure in potential renters. You might be able to negotiate months of free rent or even rent month-to-month, instead of signing a long-term lease. Renting can also cost less on a monthly basis when compared to the average mortgage payment in your area. And don't forget to add the cost of repairs, maintenance, insurance, and property taxes for a bought home. Deferred maintenance on a home can keep you up at night worrying about whether the air conditioner or the roof will last another year if you're short on money to pay for such major repairs.

Renting may also be a good choice if you have poor credit. It should come as no surprise that your credit score plays a big role in getting approved for a mortgage. A low credit score could also be a barrier to being approved for a lease, depending on whether the landlord runs a credit check on potential tenants. If your credit isn't good, consider renting from an independent owner rather than in a large apartment community, where a credit check is likely to be a part of the approval process.

Renting is also ideal if you don't know how long you'll want to live somewhere. Maybe you're just getting settled in your first job or had to relocate for a job transfer. Buying and selling property involves expenses such as real estate agent commissions, title insurance, inspection fees, moving expenses, and the various costs involved with getting a mortgage. A property must have significant value appreciation to cover those expenses, and it's not wise to bank on that happening within a relatively short period of time. If you need to pick up and move due to career or family demands, there's

Here's a quick and dirty tip: When you're not certain if you'll stay for at least five years, it makes sense to rent even if you can afford to buy a home.

nothing better than being a tenant. All you need to do is give notice according to the terms of your lease.

Apartment living usually appeals to people who like the security or the social aspect of living close to other people. An active apartment community is a great way to meet people and may have some nice amenities to enjoy at no additional charge such as a pool, a clubhouse, tennis courts, or an exercise room. If you use any of those kinds of amenities, consider what you'd have to pay for them if you weren't living there as a tenant. Plus, if you're a busy professional, not having to tend to the yard or exterior property maintenance can help keep you focused on your career.

Cons for Renting

The biggest downside to renting is that you lack control of the property, which may impact your enjoyment of it. For instance, the owner may not be responsive when repairs are needed or you may feel the general upkeep of the place gets neglected. The landlord may decide to sell the property or to increase your rent. Your lease may limit you from decorating the way you'd like, getting a pet, keeping an additional vehicle, having a relative live with you, and more. Always read a lease very carefully to make sure you understand what's allowed and what's forbidden. Breaking the terms of your lease may result in an eviction as well as having to kiss your

Here's a quick and dirty tip: Use the Rent vs. Buy Calculator at dinky town.com to help you see what taxes, fees, and monthly payments you need to consider before making the decision to buy or rent a home. Remember that insurance and property taxes can change from year to year.

deposit money good-bye. You have to decide what you're willing to compromise in exchange for the benefits that come with renting.

Pros for Buying

Even though owning a home can be expensive, it doesn't have to cost more than renting. Buying an affordable home with a reasonable mortgage can actually cost less on a monthly basis, depending on where you live. The best way to make a comparison is to analyze the monthly numbers for comparable properties. Thankfully, there are some great online calculators that can thoroughly crunch the numbers for you, like the Rent vs. Buy Calculator at dinkytown. com. But remember that a calculator can't predict the future. It estimates variables such as inflation and home appreciation. A calculator can't estimate the impact of interest rates on a decision to rent or buy. For example, if you buy a home and interest rates decrease significantly, you could refinance your mortgage and reap additional savings. That could tip the comparison to the side of home ownership, but that's very difficult to forecast.

A major benefit of owning a home is that you can build equity if you have a mortgage that amortizes. Amortization means that each monthly payment is made up of a principal and interest portion. Principal pays down your original loan amount and interest is the price you pay for having borrowed the money. For a fixed-rate mortgage, the monthly payment stays the same but the amount of principal and interest changes each month. In the early years of a fixed-rate mortgage, payments are mostly interest and very little principal. For example, on a $100,000 mortgage with a fixed 6 percent interest rate, the monthly payment is $599.55. Consider how the ratio of interest to principal differs from the beginning to the middle to the end of a thirty-year mortgage:

- The very first payment is broken down into $500 for interest and $99.55 for principal.
- The 180th payment is made up of $356.46 for interest and $243.09 for principal.

- The last payment is $2.98 for interest and $593.58 for principal—which zeros out the loan balance.

As your loan balance gets smaller, so does the amount of interest you owe, so that's why the principal portion increases at the same time that the interest portion decreases. As you build equity in a home, it makes the long-term cost of ownership less expensive than renting a comparable property. Having a home that's paid-for can be a strategy to create financial flexibility in retirement. With a paid-for home, you have the option to (1) live there, (2) sell it and downsize to a less expensive home, or (3) sell it, bank the cash, and become a renter.

Another advantage of home ownership over renting is the benefit of appreciation. If you sold a home in 2005 or 2006, you probably took advantage of the highest real estate values the United States has ever experienced. But the loud pop we heard when the real estate bubble burst was a reminder that extraordinary inflation of home prices isn't normal or economically healthy. Values have declined significantly since that time in many areas. However, if you've owned a home since 2000 or so, the current market value of the property could still be 20 percent to 40 percent higher than your purchase price. Since having a place to live is a basic human need, owning real estate is a relatively safe investment when handled judiciously.

Because the government encourages home ownership, there are some tax advantages that come with paying mortgage interest, mortgage insurance, property taxes, and some closing costs. Those tax deductions reduce the amount of income on which your taxes are calculated. I'll include a section at the end of this chapter for more about the Home Mortgage Interest Tax Deduction.

Cons for Buying

The unpleasant part of owning a home is that repairs and upkeep cost money and time. Unexpected repairs can be needed when you can least afford them. You have to schedule the repairs and perhaps take time off from work to oversee them. If you lost your income and were unable to make timely mortgage payments, you risk losing your home through a foreclosure. Foreclosure is the forced sale of a home by a lender when the terms of a mortgage are violated. A foreclosure is much more damaging to your credit rating than being evicted from a rental property for not paying rent.

WHAT CAN YOU AFFORD?

I was a real estate salesperson early in my career and witnessed the emotions that typical home buyers experience. They conjure up a vision of their future life in a home while they're seeing it for the first time. I saw many buyers willingly overpay for real estate that was going to be a huge stretch for their level of income. However, I worked with some buyers who took a more businesslike approach. They saw homes as "sticks and bricks."

They were looking for value and location more than an image they thought a particular property would convey about them. The most practical customers had no problem throwing out a low offer that was sometimes so low I was embarrassed to present it to the seller. But the tough customers taught me that when you draw a hard line about what you're willing to pay, you might get it. If the seller scoffs or has harsh words about your offer with you or your agent, my advice is to simply tell yourself *it wasn't meant to be* and move on to the next property of interest. When it comes to negotiation it's always said that he who cares the least has the upper hand.

How Much Can You Borrow?

A loan that an individual or business takes out to buy real estate is generally called a mortgage. However, there are actually two parts to a real estate loan: a mortgage and a promissory note:

1. **A mortgage** is a legal document that creates a lien on a property in order to secure a debt. The borrower is called the mortgagor and the lender is the mortgagee. When you sign a

mortgage as a home buyer, you pledge your home to the lender as collateral. If you stop making payments on the promissory note, the mortgage is what gives the lender the ability to foreclose on your property. A foreclosure allows the lender to sell the property in order to generate income to offset your outstanding debt.

2. **A promissory note** is the contract between a lender and a borrower in which the borrower agrees to repay a loan. It specifies the amount of the loan and all the terms of repayment.

A general rule of thumb for many years has been that you can afford a mortgage loan up to three times the amount of your annual household income. But that guideline is much too general to be taken as a firm rule—every buyer has unique financial circumstances. Lenders in the postcredit-crisis marketplace have tightened up their formulas and scrutinize potential borrowers more carefully. The maximum amount a lender will loan for a home depends on a combination of these factors:

- the buyer's monthly income,
- the buyer's income history,
- the buyer's existing monthly debts,
- the buyer's credit score,
- the interest rate to be charged on borrowed funds,
- the market value of the property.

There are some online resources to get an idea about how much you can afford to spend on a home. But even if a mortgage lender or an online calculator indicates that you can afford a certain amount of mortgage debt, be skeptical about whether you should borrow the maximum amount. The formula a lender or calculator uses doesn't take your entire financial situation into consideration. For example, a lender wouldn't know if you're saving enough for retirement or will be left with an ample emergency fund after you make a large down payment. Also, think about the additional expenses that owning a new home may trigger, such as buying

Here's a quick and dirty tip: Never go shopping for real estate until you have a written preapproval or loan commitment letter from a lender. That ensures you know the maximum amount to spend and shows that you're a serious and qualified buyer. Commitments also lock in a lower interest rate when rates are trending up.

furniture, artwork, remodeling costs, higher utilities, and landscaping. You have to make the decision about how much house you can afford within the context of all your other financial goals.

MORTGAGE OPTIONS

When people say, "Your home is the most expensive purchase you'll make your entire life," what they should really say is that a mortgage is probably the most expensive loan you'll pay for in your lifetime. Even if you don't intend to live in your home or own an investment property for the full length of the loan, you'll still pay a hefty amount of interest. Because mortgage amounts are so large, they're one of the most important financial decisions you'll make. That means you should take mortgage shopping very seriously and let each potential lender know that you're not going to settle for less than the best product they have to offer. Always remember to shop, compare, and negotiate for a loan with the lowest settlement costs and interest rate. You may find potential lenders in your local newspaper, on the Internet, or as referrals from friends or real estate professionals. Interest rates and points can change on a daily basis—take a look at the mortgage comparison tool at bankrate.com that shows current rates offered by major lenders.

I know shopping for a loan takes time and effort. But not shopping could cost you many thousands of dollars! Consider this: A thirty-year mortgage for $150,000 at 5 percent interest instead of 6 percent, for example, could save you as much as $30,000 in total interest over the life of the loan. Even if you decide to sell the prop-

Here's a quick and dirty tip: Download a mortgage shopping worksheet from federalreserve.gov/pubs/mortgage/worksheet.pdf. Fill it out as you speak with lenders or mortgage brokers in person or over the phone, or get information online. Then compare offers and negotiate for the best deal possible.

erty or refinance the loan after ten years, a one percent interest rate reduction would save you over $14,000. That's a savings worth shopping around for!

I discussed your credit score in chapter 5—you'll want to make sure your credit rating is as good as it can be before applying for a loan. If there are errors on your credit report, get them corrected right away. Remember that a higher credit score helps you get approved for a loan with a lower interest rate, which translates into big-time savings.

MORTGAGE LENDER VERSUS BROKER

Many people are confused about the difference between a mortgage lender and a mortgage broker. Mortgage brokers don't actually lend their own money, but instead connect borrowers with various mortgage lenders. Brokers can be an employee of a firm or work as an independent. They must hold a professional broker's license in most states. The typical duties of a mortgage broker include counseling customers, checking credit, verifying application documents, matching borrowers with appropriate financial products, locking in interest rates and terms with lenders, arranging for appraisals, providing required legal disclosures, and ensuring that the lender's funds get disbursed at closing. After the real estate purchase is completed, any questions about the mortgage go to the lender, not to the mortgage broker.

I've used mortgage brokers to get loans for all kinds of real estate very successfully. They can expedite the buying process because they know who to go to for special circumstances such as an investor loan for a rental property. A well-connected mortgage broker can be a huge asset to finding the best deal on a mortgage. They're familiar with all the various mortgage products and can provide creative solutions for your individual situation. Brokers are usually paid on a commission basis, which can come from the borrower, the lender, or from both. But their compensation can also come from an increase in the interest rate or as "points" paid at closing. I'll give you more information about points coming up.

MORTGAGE TYPES

There are three basic types of mortgages that you should be familiar with: fixed-rate, adjustable-rate, and interest-only.

1. **A fixed-rate mortgage** has an interest rate and monthly payment that never changes. The length of a typical fixed-rate loan is 30 years, but you can also choose 10-, 15-, 20-, and even 40- or 50-year mortgages. A portion of each payment goes toward both paying down the debt and paying interest. But the proportion of principal and interest within the fixed payment changes each month. That's because as the principal balance amortizes or decreases, so does the amount of interest you pay. But since the monthly payment stays the same, the excess is subtracted from the principal balance each month, helping you build increasing equity in your home. Take a look at how the payment is split up for the first six months on a thirty-year fixed-rate mortgage of $200,000 at 6 percent interest:

PAYMENT MONTH	BEGINNING BALANCE (each month is reduced by the prior month's principal portion paid)	MONTHLY FIXED PAYMENT	INTEREST PORTION (6% of each month's beginning balance)	PRINCIPAL PORTION ($1,199 payment minus the month's interest portion)
1	$200,000	$1,199	$1,000	$199
2	$199,801	$1,199	$999	$200
3	$199,601	$1,199	$998	$201
4	$199,400	$1,199	$997	$202
5	$199,198	$1,199	$996	$203
6	$198,995	$1,199	$995	$204

The following amortization chart shows the annual proportion of principal and interest for this same loan over the full thirty-year term. Since the fixed monthly payment is $1,199, the annual amount is $14,388 ($1,199×12).

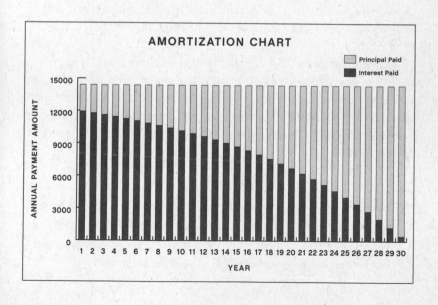

As you can see, the portion of a fixed-rate mortgage payment that's credited to the principal balance increases slowly in the early years, but picks up steam in the later years. And conversely, the interest you pay early in the loan is proportionately high but gets significantly lowered in the later years.

2. **Adjustable-rate mortgages** are known as ARMs, and their terms and conditions vary. The core of the product is that the interest rate adjusts or fluctuates up or down from its start rate. That can happen monthly, semiannually, annually or not at all until after a certain period of time. There are limits, or caps, on how much the interest rate can increase over a given amount of time as well as over the life of the loan. A typical cap might be an increase of 2 percent per year and 6 percent over the life of the loan. Option ARMs adjust based on a variety of payment options and index rates that a borrower chooses. An index is a statistical benchmark—when it moves up or down, an adjustable-rate mortgage that's linked to it moves accordingly. A couple of common indices for mortgages are the Treasury bill rates and the London Interbank Offered Rate (LIBOR). Since mortgage payments count for a large portion of most homeowners' monthly spending, it's important to fully understand when and by how much your ARM payment can change.

3. **An interest-only loan** is the third type of mortgage. It charges a monthly payment that is 100 percent interest. In addition to the three basic mortgage types, there are many different hybrid loans that combine features. For instance, an interest-only loan usually converts to either a fixed- or adjustable-rate mortgage after a certain period of time.

 Here's a quick and dirty tip: Before you agree to an index for an adjustable-rate mortgage, look at its track record over the past few years to see how your payment would have fluctuated. Consider that the index could be more volatile in the future.

MORTGAGE CATEGORIES

There are three broad categories of loans in the residential lending market:

- **Conventional** loans are created by private corporations and don't have any government underwriting or guarantee that back them up in case the borrower doesn't pay. Different types of conventional loans include fixed-rate, adjustable-rate, and interest-only. They usually require Private Mortgage Insurance (PMI) to be rolled into the monthly payment for loans that exceed 80 percent of the property's market value.

- **Federal Housing Administration (FHA)** loans are made by FHA-approved lenders and are insured by the federal government. They offer a low down payment for those who may not meet conventional loan requirements or who have experienced a foreclosure or bankruptcy. Different types of FHA loans include fixed-rate, adjustable-rate, and graduated payments (where payments start small and increase gradually over time). The most popular FHA loan is the 203(b) fixed-rate because it allows financing up to 97 percent with closing costs that can be paid by someone other than the borrower. All closing costs on a 203(b) can be a gift from a relative, a nonprofit, or a government agency. Visit fha.com and hud.gov for more details on FHA products and guidelines.

- **Department of Veterans Affairs (VA)** loans are available to veterans (and their surviving spouses, in certain cases) and active duty military personnel and members of the reserves and the National Guard. The loan is made by a VA-approved lender and is guaranteed by the VA even in situations where a borrower has poor credit or has experienced a bankruptcy. The borrower can finance 100 percent with low closing costs and no monthly mortgage insurance payment. Different types of VA loans include fixed-rate and adjustable-rate. For more information go to home loans.va.gov or veteransservices.com.

Here's a quick and dirty tip: Private Mortgage Insurance (PMI) is added to your payment when you get a conventional mortgage that's more than 80 percent of the property's value. Once you believe your loan balance is below 80 percent of the value, notify your lender and request that they stop charging you PMI premiums.

CHOOSING A MORTGAGE

I've mentioned how important it is to shop around for a mortgage you'll want to live with. The type of loan (fixed, adjustable, or interest-only) you choose should fit with your financial situation. If your income fluctuates or you don't want to take on much financial risk, a fixed-rate mortgage is best for you. Fixed payments make it easy to create a long-term spending plan. Adjustable-rate loans may look attractive if the interest rate is low today, but if you can't afford future rate increases, you could get into financial trouble later on.

That's exactly what happened to many people who have been forced into foreclosure during the recent financial crisis. The adjustable start rate, also known as the teaser rate, of their loan was affordable for a while. But as rates adjusted up and the recession caused many to lose their jobs or experience major cuts in income, a perfect storm for financial wreckage was brewing. Unfortunately, financing 95 percent to 100 percent of a home's inflated market value at an adjustable rate became commonplace. When considering an adjustable-rate mortgage, be sure to find out the maximum amount it can increase—that's called the lifetime cap. If you can't afford the highest possible monthly payment, think twice about whether an adjustable-rate loan is best for you.

However, if you're confident that you can weather any payment increase that may occur with an adjustable-rate mortgage, you can get a lower interest rate when compared to a fixed-rate loan. The lower interest rate for an adjustable is usually locked in for the first few years. So if you plan on having the loan for a relatively short period of time, an adjustable loan will usually save you money. If you keep an adjustable mortgage for a long time, consider that the interest rate can go up, but come back down—or perhaps never go up at all. It's wise to borrow less than you can or to have a reserve fund to draw from in case adjustable rates swell and make your payment unaffordable. Don't count on always being able to refinance a loan or to sell your property if you're caught in a tight spot.

The Many Mortgage Fees

A big part of comparing mortgages is to analyze their various fees. Be familiar with the following:

- **Interest rate** or note rate is the annual amount you pay for borrowing money.

- **Annual percentage rate (APR)** is an important way to compare a mortgage's overall cost. APR combines a loan's interest with the other fees charged by a lender (such as points, mortgage broker fees, and origination fees) and expresses them as an annual percentage. So the APR should always be higher than the interest rate because it includes loan costs in addition to the annual interest rate. The Truth in Lending Act requires lenders to disclose the APR so they can't advertise low interest rates that actually hide their fees. However, the APR isn't as useful for adjustable-rate mortgages because future interest rate changes can't be predicted. Nor does the APR take into account costs you must pay third party companies involved in your real estate purchase for costs such as inspections, a survey, or a real estate commission, for example. Get a list of which fees are included in an APR calculation from a potential lender.

- **Discount points** are fees paid to the lender that equals one percent of the loan amount. For example, one point on a $200,000 loan costs $2,000. Paying points is a way to "buy down" your interest rate because the more points you pay up front, the lower your interest rate will be, and that saves money over the life of the loan. Plus, points are generally tax deductible, so they lower your taxable income (even if the seller pays part or all of them for

> Here's a quick and dirty tip: To know if you should pay points, ask what the monthly payment would be with paying points and without them. Take the difference between the two payments and divide it into the points charged. That calculates your break-even point: how many months you need to stay in the home to benefit from paying points.

you). If you plan to keep your mortgage for at least a few years, and can afford it, paying points can be worth it.

- **Origination fees:** the cost a lender charges to process your application. Some lenders may return this fee to you at closing if you're approved and decide to take their loan.
- **Credit report fee:** the fee a lender pays one or several of the major credit bureaus to obtain copies of your credit report.
- **Survey:** a lender hires a surveyor to confirm the location of buildings, boundaries, and easements on the property.
- **Appraisal:** a lender hires a certified appraiser to determine the value of the property.
- **Title search:** verifies that there are no "clouds" on the title or liens that must be cleared up before you can take ownership.
- **Title insurance:** protects the lender in case another party claims legal title or interest in the property that secures their loan to you.
- **Mortgage broker commission:** the cost a broker charges to match you with a lender, process your paperwork, and overseeing the funding of your purchase. Some lenders may allow you to roll all or a portion of your settlement costs into your total loan amount. That increases your principal loan balance, monthly payments, and may also increase your interest rate. A lender is required to give you a good faith estimate (GFE) within three days after receiving your loan application, which lists all of the expected fees. It includes the lender's fees in ad-

dition to estimated third party fees such as title insurance and the appraisal. It's always possible to negotiate some of the lender's charges down or to ask for them to be waived completely.

Real Estate Settlement Fees

Other settlement fees that you may be charged at a real estate closing:

- **Recording fees:** charged by the county to record your mortgage and deed documents for the public records.
- **Property taxes:** depending on the date of your purchase you may have to reimburse the seller for taxes they've already paid.
- **Homeowners insurance:** lenders generally require you to have insurance at closing and to prepay six months' to a year's worth of coverage.
- **Escrow fees:** charged by the company or attorney who facilitates the closing. They ensure that the terms of a real estate contract are fulfilled, do legal research on the title, receive funding, and pay all the parties in full.
- **Inspections:** you must settle up with companies who performed home inspections such as engineering, pest, septic system, wells, and water quality, for example.
- **Real estate agent or attorney:** you must pay any fee or commission that you agreed to pay a real estate agent or attorney.
- **Homeowner association dues:** depending on the date of your purchase you may have to reimburse the seller for dues they've already paid in advance.

QUESTIONS TO ASK A POTENTIAL LENDER

1. How much down payment do you require?
2. Will you require Private Mortgage Insurance (PMI)? If so, how much will that add to the monthly payment?
3. Will you guarantee your good faith estimate?

4. Will you offer a written loan commitment that locks in an interest rate if rates are trending up? If so, for how long and for how much?
5. Will you charge a prepayment penalty when I sell the property, pay off any portion of the loan early, or do a refinance? If so, for how long and for how much?
6. How much time does it take to get approved and funded?

TAKING THE HOME MORTGAGE INTEREST DEDUCTION

When you borrow money to buy, build, or substantially improve your primary residence or a second home, you get a tax break. The interest paid on mortgage balances up to one million dollars is a tax-deductible expense. And interest paid on up to $100,000 of home equity loans or lines of credit is generally tax deductible, too. In addition to mortgage interest, there are a few more expenses and fees you can include in the deduction, such as late payment fees, prepayment penalties, mortgage insurance premiums, and discount points. At the end of the year your lender will send you Form 1098, which is a Mortgage Interest Statement. To claim the home mortgage interest deduction, enter the total amount of qualifying interest and fees on Schedule A of Tax Form 1040.

Who Qualifies to Take the Deduction?

There are four conditions that must be met in order to qualify to take the home mortgage interest deduction:

1. You must file your taxes on Form 1040 and itemize your deductions. That means you list each of your tax-deductible expenses like charitable contributions, medical costs, and state and local taxes, instead of taking the default standard deduction. (See more about tax deductions in chapter 10.)
2. You must be a bona fide borrower with an arm's length relationship to your lender. In other words, if your creditor is a

close family member or a friend, taking the interest deduction
could be suspect.

3. Your mortgage must be a secured debt, which means that the
   loan is backed by real estate that could be sold to protect the
   interests of the lender if you don't repay the debt.

4. You must be legally liable for the loan. So if you pay for someone else's mortgage, you're not eligible to deduct any portion
   of the mortgage interest on your tax return.

Homes That Qualify for the Deduction

For the purpose of the home mortgage interest deduction, the definition of a "home" includes just about any property with a bathroom,
kitchen, and a sleeping area, such as a house, condo, co-op, town-
home, mobile home, trailer, or boat. If you own a second home, it
may also be eligible for the interest deduction. However, there are
special rules that you must follow if you rent it out during any part
of the year.

A second home that's also a rental must be used personally by
you for more than fourteen days or more than 10 percent of the
number of days that the home is rented by others, whichever is longer. For example, let's say you own a beach house and rent it out
from June 1 through August 31 when the weather's too hot for you
to enjoy it. That means you rent out the beach house for 92 days of
the year, so 10 percent of 92 equals 9 days. The fourteen-day requirement is longer than nine days, so as long as you use the beach house
for more than fourteen days of the year, you can consider it a true
second home, eligible for the mortgage interest deduction. Otherwise, the beach house would be considered a rental property, subject
to tax rules for rental properties rather than for personal residences.

Mortgage Interest and Multiple Borrowers

If you buy a home with your spouse and file taxes together, you
claim the total amount of qualified mortgage interest on your joint
return. However, if you're married and file taxes separately, or you
borrowed money to buy a home with someone who isn't your spouse,

you each get to take a deduction for the interest you paid. If the Mortgage Interest Statement was mailed to another borrower and you didn't receive one, simply send a document with your tax return that explains how much interest each of the borrowers paid. It's a good idea to include the name and address of the person who did receive the Mortgage Interest Statement in your explanation. If you own a home or a portion of a home, be sure to deduct your allowable mortgage interest. It's important to take every tax deduction that you can because each one lowers your taxable income, which reduces the amount of taxes you have to pay.

If you're considering making the leap from tenant to home owner, it's smart to be as prepared as possible. It's a decision not to be entered into lightly because it can turn out to be your castle or your prison, depending on your situation!

9

Paying for Education

> Education is a progressive discovery of our own ignorance.
> —WILL DURANT, writer and historian

It's likely that, in addition to buying a home, one of your goals has to do with paying for education. Higher education is an important investment in our future—but the cost of tuition and room and board at colleges keeps rising year after year. Even the cost of private elementary and high school can make you shudder. That gives parents and potential students a lot of anxiety about what quality of education they'll be able to afford. How you'll pay for your own education, or that of a child, depends on your unique situation.

If you have young children, it's difficult to know exactly how much college will cost when they'll be ready to go. There are financial aid options such as scholarships, fellowships, grants, loans, and work-study programs for post-secondary education. But getting those types of assistance depends on various factors such as income, assets, and the student's academic, athletic, or civic achievements at the time they're ready to apply to college. There are thousands of scholarships and grant opportunities in the private and public sector depending on the student's area of academic interest. In this chapter, I'll give you tips and resources to help make paying for education more manageable for you or your children.

CREATE AN EDUCATION SAVINGS PLAN

I recommend saving for a child's education only after you have accomplished the following:

1. Built up your family's emergency cash fund to a minimum of three months' worth of living expenses
2. Created and are consistently funding an adequate retirement savings plan

If you sacrifice your own financial security for the education of one or several children, you may find yourself relying on them to support you in your old age! That isn't a good trade-off for you or your children. You have to provide for your own financial well-being, even if that means contributing less than you'd like to for their education. Unfortunately, there aren't any grants or federal loans for retirees. When your children are accepted to school, they can take advantage of educational assistance and, if necessary, earn money to pay for their education.

If you want to pay for all or a substantial amount of your child(ren)'s education, you'll need to make it a part of your spending plan. You may even need to work longer than you planned or take on a second job to supplement your income. Paying for education costs with money earmarked for retirement means it won't be there for you when you need it. If you're in a position to help your children later on, you can always gift them money to pay down their student loans.

However, when it comes to saving for your own education, I recommend you make that goal a top priority, not because you're more important than your children. It's because achieving your educational goals sooner rather than later is beneficial for you and your family. Getting your chosen degree is an investment in yourself and in your financial future. With a diploma in hand, you'll have the skills, abilities, and credentials to earn more, pay off student loans, and save regularly for your retirement.

THE PLAN OF THIRDS

One way to plan for your own education or that of a child is to divide up the goal into thirds. Let's say you want to complete a graduate program that costs $30,000. Consider this savings and payment goal:

1. Save $10,000 before you start school
2. Earn $10,000 by working while you attend school
3. Pay off the final $10,000 as loan payments after you graduate from school

You must apply for a student loan before you start school or during your program. Most student loans have built-in deferment of payments until six months following graduation. So you can secure a loan at the beginning of your education, but pay it off over the long term after your joyous graduation!

As part of your education plan, it's a good strategy to apply to a variety of schools including one or two that are relatively inexpensive. That way, if you can't save enough or get sufficient financial aid to pay for a pricey school, you'll still have options!

No matter how much you're able to squirrel away for education, it's wise to use tax-advantaged education savings accounts or ESAs. There are two ESAs to be familiar with: 529 plans and Coverdells.

USE 529 EDUCATION SAVINGS PLANS

A 529 savings plan is also known as a Qualified Tuition Program. It's an investment vehicle that's become the most popular way to save for higher education. The idea is that you contribute money to the plan that can be used to pay for a student's qualified expenses at a specific, eligible school such as a college, university, vocational school, or other postsecondary school that participates in federal student aid. A 529 plan can be opened for any adult or child in your family or even outside of your family.

529 Prepaid Plans

Plans known as 529s are generally categorized as either prepaid plans or savings plans. Prepaid plans are offered by schools and allow you to prepay all or a portion of the future cost. That means you're paying for future education at today's prices—what a bargain! If the student decides to attend a different eligible school, the funds can still be used for qualified expenses. However, depending on which plan you have, there may be a penalty for transferring funds to another plan.

529 Savings Plans

The 529 savings plans, on the other hand, are similar to a retirement account where your contributions are invested in chosen mutual funds or securities. The account value will fluctuate based on the performance of the underlying investments. That means your funds could increase enough to outpace the rising costs of tuition, or they could fall short.

Either type of 529 plan can be set up by individual states, and each one determines the structure of its plan and which investment options will be offered. However, a qualified institution can usually only offer a prepaid plan. The school you're interested in can tell you if they're eligible to accept 529 funds and if they operate their own plan. But if they don't operate one, don't worry, every state now has at least one 529 plan in which you can participate.

Which 529 Plan Is Best?

Enrollment in a 529 can be done directly with the plan manager or through an independent stockbroker or financial advisor. Each plan has different features and benefits, so it's important to do some research before enrolling in one. There's a great 529 savings plan comparison tool at savingforcollege.com. While you're there, check out the look-up tool for 529 eligible schools.

Many people believe that if they contribute to a state 529 plan, that the student must attend a school in that state. In most plans you can choose any school no matter where you live or what state or institution manages the plan! You could live in California, invest in a Florida plan, but send a student to a North Carolina college. So don't fall for the misconception that a state-sponsored 529 plan is only for those who want to send a student to a state school.

Benefits of 529 Plans

The 529 plans offer some nice savings because contributions and earnings grow tax-free. Funds in a 529 are taxed only if withdrawals from the account exceed the total amount of qualified education expenses. You may be able to receive some additional tax advantages if you invest in a plan sponsored by your home state. Another reason 529s are so popular is because they offer flexibility. You can generally roll over funds from one plan to another within sixty days without incurring a penalty. And the student, who's called the designated beneficiary, can always be changed to another member of the beneficiary's family, so if the child you're saving for decides to become the next world-champion bass fisherman instead of going to college, no worries!

There are no income or age restrictions placed on contributors or students. Everyone is eligible to take advantage of a 529 plan. The maximum amount you can contribute actually varies from plan to plan, but it's over $300,000 per student in many state plans. There's no annual limit to how much you can contribute. However, contributions can't exceed the amount of educational expenses that the student will need. If you're not sure how to calculate that amount, contact the eligible school for a total estimate of qualified costs for the student.

Qualified expenses that can be paid with 529 savings include tuition, fees, books, and all required equipment and supplies for coursework. Reasonable costs for room and board also qualify for those who are at least half-time students.

USE COVERDELL EDUCATION SAVINGS ACCOUNTS

Coverdell ESAs are another tax-advantaged account that can be used to save for any level of education, from kindergarten through graduate school. They're similar to an IRA in that you have many different investment choices and the funds grow tax-free. (In fact, they used to be called Education IRAs.) But Coverdells differ from 529 plans in that they have more restrictions, such as limitations on who can contribute, how much can be contributed each year, and the age of the student who'll use the funds.

Coverdells can be opened with traditional or online brokerages as well as with many banks and mutual fund companies. You'll find a list of low-cost Coverdell providers at savingforcollege.com. The account must be opened for a designated beneficiary who's under the age of eighteen. After the student's eighteenth birthday, no more contributions can be made unless the account is for a special-needs beneficiary. The funds must generally be used by the time the student reaches age thirty in order to avoid taxes and penalties.

Benefits of Coverdells

With both Coverdells and 529 plans, your contributions and earnings grow tax-free as long as distributions are used to pay for qualified expenses at eligible schools. That could be any postsecondary school—such as a university or college—that's eligible to participate in federal student aid.

WHAT HAPPENS IF YOU SAVE TOO MUCH?

What if you can't use all the Coverdell or 529 plan funds for the beneficiary's qualified expenses? Maybe the student graduates with all her education bills paid, but there's still $1,000 left in the account. If the leftover money is withdrawn, it will generally be considered a taxable distribution, also subject to an additional 10 percent tax penalty. Instead of closing the account and taking a taxable distribution, change the designated beneficiary to a member of the student's family who's a potential student. That can include siblings, step-relatives, and cousins of the student, for example.

The unique feature of Coverdells is that they can be used to pay for the expenses of younger students, which includes children in kindergarten through grade twelve who attend any eligible public, private, or religious school. There are a few more qualified expenses for younger students than for those getting postsecondary education. They include tuition, fees, books, supplies, computer equipment, Internet access, academic tutoring, uniforms, transportation, and room and board. Any school you're interested in can tell you if they're eligible to accept Coverdell funds.

You can contribute to a Coverdell savings account only if your adjusted gross income is less than $110,000 or less than $220,000 if you file a joint tax return. Companies and trusts are even allowed to make contributions to Coverdells, no matter how much income they earn. There's an annual contribution limit of $2,000 per student. The limit applies even if more than one Coverdell account has been opened or more than one person makes contributions for the same beneficiary. Contribution thresholds can change over time, so it's best to check the IRS website for the most up-to-date information at irs.gov.

Consider this scenario:

After Baby Elizabeth is born, her parents decide to set up a Coverdell for her and her grandparents also decide to set one up. That's fine as long as the total contributions for the child to both her Coverdell accounts don't exceed $2,000 per year. If her parents contribute $500 and her grandparents contribute $1,500, together they have maxed out the allowable yearly limit for Baby Elizabeth.

Here's a quick and dirty tip: If you earn too much to contribute to a Coverdell, gift the money to the student, and help them open up the account for themselves.

If you want to save more than $2,000 a year for a child's education, you can also open and contribute to a 529 plan for them in the same year. The deadline for making Coverdell contributions is the due date for filing your tax return for the prior year. (There is no deadline for making 529 plan contributions.) Coverdells are great if you're saving for a younger child's elementary or high school education. But when you're saving just for college expenses, consider the advantages of the 529 plan. As I mentioned, 529 savings plans have no limit for annual contributions and offer more flexibility than Coverdells when saving for higher education.

The following chart compares the major features of the 529 and Coverdell Education Savings accounts:

FEATURE	529 ESA	COVERDELL ESA*
Age of student who will use funds	Can be any age	Must be younger than 18 and use the funds by age 30
Contribution limit per student	No limit, but must not exceed the qualified expenses	$2,000
Qualified school	Any eligible postsecondary institution	Generally any public or private institution from kindergarten to graduate school
Age of contributor	No age restriction	No age restriction
Income limit of individual contributor	No income restriction	$220,000 for Married filing jointly / $110,000 for others

FEATURE	529 ESA	COVERDELL ESA*
Qualified expenses	Tuition, fees, books, equipment, and supplies for coursework, reasonable room and board, plus computer and related technology and Internet access	Tuition, fees, books, equipment, and supplies for coursework, tutoring, uniforms, reasonable room and board, transportation (Computer, related technology, and Internet access are currently qualified expenses for 2009–2010 only.)
Contributions are tax-deductible	No	No
Taxation of investment earnings	Growth is tax-free	Growth is tax-free
Taxation of withdrawals	Occurs only if distributions exceed the amount of qualified education expenses	Occurs only if distributions exceed the amount of qualified education expenses
Deadline for contributions	None	Tax return due date

*Special note: As I write this, the future of Coverdells is uncertain. It's possible that some of the advantages of the program may expire at the end of 2010. If that happens, Coverdells will exist, but several of their key benefits will cease to exist. For example, the amount you can contribute will be cut and K–12 expenses will no longer qualify. If the latter happens, 529s will be a superior choice. Check finaid.org or savingforcollege.com for the most up-to-date information.

MAKE TUITION MORE AFFORDABLE

In addition to building your own college savings plan, you should also consider ways to lower the cost of a college education. Here are four general ways to make the cost of education more affordable:

1. **Take advantage of gifts.** If you have family members who know that you're trying to save for your own education or that of a child's, they may be willing to help out. Consider tactfully offering them

the option to substitute birthday and holiday presents for education money.

2. **Get tuition reimbursement.** If you're considering going back to school and paying for your own education while you continue to work, approach your employer about your eligibility for tuition reimbursement. Workplace educational assistance programs allow you to exclude up to $5,250 from your taxable income for those benefits received each year. Some companies have a formal policy with strings attached, such as how long you have to stay employed once you accept tuition reimbursement. They also may only pay for coursework directly related to your current job.

If your company doesn't reimburse tuition as a company benefit, you still may be able to get some assistance. Create a business proposal that outlines the program you plan to complete, its full cost, and why getting the education will make you a more valuable employee to the company. That's how I was able to secure about a third of the funds to pay for my MBA program. Even though I worked for a Fortune 500 company that had no tuition benefit, I was able to demonstrate that the education would increase my value to the company and to our customers. I completed a weekend program for professionals over several years that allowed me to continue working full-time.

3. **Consider private awards.** There are thousands of grants, scholarships, and fellowships available in the private sector from individuals, organizations, and corporations. They don't have to be paid back and are tax-free if you're a candidate for a degree and use the funds for qualified expenses (tuition and required fees related to coursework) at an eligible institution. However, they're considered taxable income if the money is used for nonqualified expenses. High school guidance counselors and college financial aid offices usually have a list of potential local and national organizations with money to give away for education. Conduct Internet searches and do research at sites like:

- collegeanswer.com
- ecampustours.com

- fulbright.state.gov
- fastweb.com
- collegescholarships.org
- studentaid.ed.gov
- usafunds.org

4. Get low-cost private funding. If you can't get any type of aid or you need to borrow an additional amount to foot your education bill, there are low-cost private loan options. There's a growing online network at TuitionU.com that introduces students to a community of unique and low-cost alternatives such as peer-to-peer lending, not-for-profit credit unions, sponsors, charitable donors, as well as traditional lenders. The site also has resources to help you plan, budget, and get advice from experts and other students on the best ways to pay for higher education.

5. Don't forget about federal student financial aid. The cornerstone to getting aid is submitting the Free Application for Federal Student Aid (FAFSA). The FAFSA is required by all institutions that participate in any kind of financial aid program, so getting it submitted should be a top priority when considering how to fund your education. The FAFSA does not provide an option for applicants to explain special circumstances or financial hardships. Since financial aid eligibility is based on your income from the prior year, the FAFSA may not accurately reflect your financial situation. If your income has been substantially reduced from the prior year, it's important to document your circumstances and approach the schools' financial aid administrator. The administrator has the authority to adjust aid on a case-by-case basis by rendering a Professional Judgment, which can override the information you submit on the FAFSA.

 Here's a quick and dirty tip: Many people who think they earn too much to qualify for federal aid may still be eligible. Be sure to submit the FAFSA online at fafsa.ed.gov to find out.

FEDERAL STUDENT LOANS

When it comes time to actually start paying for college you may need to consider student loans. A federal student loan is money funded by or insured by the federal government based on the FAFSA. When you accept a student loan, you enter into a contract to repay it according to specific terms. Most education loans allow you to defer making any payments until after you graduate from school. A government-backed student loan will have the lowest interest rate with the most flexibility when compared to typical private loans. For example, federal loans give you the ability to easily consolidate multiple loans and offer deferment of payments, forbearance, and even loan cancellation if you meet specific criteria.

WHAT IS STUDENT LOAN DEFERMENT?

Student loan deferment is when a lender excuses a borrower from making payments for a period of time. It's a financial "time out" that's granted when a borrower is current with their payments, but meets certain criteria. Some common events that may qualify for deferment include becoming unemployed, disabled, pregnant, adopting a young child, having your work hours reduced, going into the military, beginning a medical internship or residency, being a student enrolled at least half-time, or going into the Peace Corps, for example. Always contact your lender to explain your situation and obtain the proper forms to document your case for deferment.

The only negative aspect of a federal student loan is that nonpayment of the debt results in serious consequences. If you default on a student loan it can be very detrimental to your credit rating—so always take an education loan very seriously and never borrow more than you can afford to pay back. Student loan is a type of debt that usually doesn't get discharged even if you file for bankruptcy. If you don't make payments on a federal student loan for more than 270 days, without making any special arrangements, it's considered to be in default. Once the U.S. Department of Education initiates collection efforts against you, they can do the following to recover their money:

- Require your employer to garnish 15 percent of your wages and forward it to them for loan repayment
- Seize your federal or state tax refund or any other payment they're authorized by law to use for loan repayment
- Charge you the costs associated with hiring a private collection agency
- Deny you terms of the loan such as deferment or forbearance
- Bring litigation against you to force loan repayment

WHAT IS STUDENT LOAN FORBEARANCE?

Student loan forbearance is when a lender allows a borrower to stop making loan payments due to a serious financial hardship. It may be available even if you've defaulted, or missed payments. Unsubsidized loans will usually continue to accrue interest during a deferment period, which can be paid monthly or added to the existing loan balance. For subsidized loans, your interest is paid by the government. Always contact your lender to explain your situation and obtain the proper forms to document your case for forbearance.

In the past there were two types of federal loans: Federal Direct Loans and Federal Family Education Loans (FFEL). Direct loans are made directly by the government and FFELs were made by private lenders but guaranteed by the government. Effective June 30, 2010, the FFEL program was eliminated so all new federal loans must be originated through the Federal Direct Loan program. This transition was made in an effort to reduce government spending by cutting out subsidies for lending middlemen.

Visit studentloanborrowerassistance.org for details about federal loan features and benefits.

WHAT IS STUDENT LOAN FORGIVENESS?

Loan forgiveness, or cancellation, is when a lender erases all or a portion of a borrower's debt in certain limited circumstances. Those might include problems with your institution such as it closing or not issuing a tuition refund. Loans can be canceled due to a borrower's death or total disability. There is also career-related eligibility for loan forgiveness such as performing military service, going into the Peace Corps or AmeriCorps, teaching low-income or disabled students, doing community service for needy populations, providing health care services, going into law enforcement, even being a relative of someone who is an eligible public servant or a victim of the 9/11 tragedy.

Categories of Federal Student Aid

Here are brief descriptions of the different categories of federal student aid that may be available to you:

- **Stafford loans** are the most popular student loan program. They're available as either a subsidized (needs-based) or unsubsidized product for undergraduates and graduate students. They have a six-month grace period following graduation before you must begin making payments. Subsidized loans allow a student to waive interest payments until six months after graduation. Unsubsidized loans require that all interest payments be made from the beginning of the loan. The interest can usually be deferred while the borrower is in school. However, when you choose to defer interest, it gets added to the principal balance of the loan when repayment begins.

 Here's a quick and dirty tip: If you would be eligible for public service loan forgiveness, but don't have a Direct Loan, consider consolidating loans into the Direct Loan program to qualify for the forgiveness benefit.

- **Grants** do not have to be paid back and are tax-free if you're a candidate for a degree and use the funds for qualified expenses (tuition and required fees related to coursework) at an eligible school. Grant money is considered taxable income if it's used for nonqualified expenses. There are different kinds of grants, such as the Pell Grant, which is based on financial need. There are many other grants that can be awarded based on a student's academic achievement or field of study.

- **School-based aid** are programs administered by a participating school. They include the Federal Perkins Loan and the Federal Work-Study (FWS) program. Perkins loans are earmarked for the most financially challenged students. Work-Study allows a student to work part-time on or off campus to offset educational expenses. Eligible schools receive a limited amount of funds to award for programs each year, so the secret to snagging school funds is to be the early bird! Be sure to submit the FAFSA or any other application required by your school as early as you can, even before you're officially accepted. The amount of aid you can get depends on how early you apply, your financial need, as well as the amount of other funds you've received.

- **Parent Loans for Undergraduate Students (PLUS)** are available for parents who want to take out a loan to fund a child's education. The program also makes loans directly to graduate students. PLUS products come with low interest rates and flexible repayment plans when compared to typical private funding options. However, unlike most other federal loans, your credit score is a factor for approval for PLUS loans.

  - Parents can submit a PLUS loan application online at parentplus-loan.com.
  - Graduate and professional degree students can submit a Grad PLUS loan application at gradloans.com. To be eligible you must be enrolled in a program at least half-time, be independent of your parents, and have good credit history. You must also file your annual FAFSA to be considered for approval.

Here's a quick and dirty tip: In addition to federal programs, the FAFSA is also required for campus-based aid, state loans, and many grant and scholarship programs. Be sure to submit it on time; otherwise you could be leaving free education money on the table!

TAX BENEFITS FOR EDUCATION

In addition to student loans and financial aid, there are other ways to help lower the costs of education that involve getting tax deductions and credits. These tax benefits are available whether you're paying for your own or someone else's education:

Tuition and Fees Tax Deduction

The tuition and fees deduction can reduce your taxable income by as much as $4,000. This deduction is for the cost of enrollment and required course-related books, supplies, and equipment. You can take it even if you don't itemize deductions on your tax return; however, there are income limits for eligibility—$80,000 or $160,000 for married couples who file a joint return. Taxpayers who are married and file separately are not eligible to claim this deduction. You take the tuition and fees deduction by submitting IRS Form 8917. Note that you can't take this deduction if you also claim an education tax credit in the same year. You must choose to take either the deduction or the credit for education expenses— the IRS doesn't allow you to double up on tax benefits.

Student Loan Interest Tax Deduction

Once you begin making payments on one or more qualified student loans for higher education, you can take a deduction for the interest you pay on them each year. The deduction doesn't apply for loans taken from a relative or from a retirement plan. The deduction can reduce your taxable income by as much as $2,500.

You're eligible to claim the deduction if your adjusted gross income doesn't exceed $75,000 or $150,000 if you're married and file jointly. You can take the student loan interest deduction even if you don't itemize deductions on your return. To claim it, there's not a separate form that you have to submit—just enter the allowable amount on your tax return.

Business Deduction for Work-Related Education

If you're an employee and itemize your deductions on your tax return, you may be eligible to claim a deduction for work-related education expenses. The education must be required by your employer or improve your skills in your current job. You're allowed to lump together education, job, or miscellaneous expenses (for which you're not reimbursed by your employer) and deduct them from your taxable income when the total exceeds 2 percent of your adjusted gross income. If you are self-employed, you may deduct education expenses related to your business from your self-employment income.

American Opportunity Tax Credit

This new credit is available for qualified expenses for higher education. It modifies the less generous Hope Credit, making it available to more taxpayers for the 2009 and 2010 tax years. The income limits to qualify have been increased to $90,000 or $180,000 for those who file jointly. The credit pays up to $2,500 for the cost of qualified tuition and related expenses such as books, supplies, and coursework materials that you pay for in 2009 and 2010. If a computer is necessary for school enrollment, it's considered a qualified cost. The credit is 40 percent refundable, which means that even if you don't owe any tax, you can still get a portion of your eligible credit as a tax refund. You claim it by submitting IRS Form 8863 with your tax return. If you choose to claim the American Opportunity tax credit, you can not also claim the Tuition and Fees Tax Deduction in the same year. Check irs.gov to find out if this credit gets extended for tax years after 2010.

Lifetime Learning Credit

This credit amount is generally $2,000 for qualified education expenses per tax return for an unlimited number of years. The student does not have to pursue a degree; they can take just one course at an eligible institution to qualify. However, you can't claim both the Lifetime Learning and the American Opportunity tax credits for the same student in one year. You're not eligible for the credit if you're married filing separately. To claim the credit you must not earn more than $60,000 or $120,000 for married couples filing jointly.

SUMMARY OF EDUCATION TAX BREAKS

Here's a list of many tax benefits related to expenses for education:

1. Receive tax-free educational reimbursement from your employer
2. Receive tax-free assistance in the form of a grant, scholarship, or fellowship
3. Use a 529 prepaid plan to pay for future college tuition at today's cost
4. Use a 529 savings plan to get tax-free growth for qualified college expenses
5. Use a Coverdell savings plan to get tax-free growth for qualified expenses for students in kindergarten through graduate school
6. Deduct tuition and educational fees from your taxable income
7. Deduct student loan interest from your taxable income
8. Deduct work-related education expenses as a business deduction
9. Take a 40 percent refundable tax credit up to $2,500 for many qualified expenses for higher education
10. Take a tax credit up to $2,000 for taking individual courses and nondegree-seeking job improvement education
11. Receive tax-free treatment of a canceled student loan

12. Take an early distribution from a retirement account for the costs of higher education with no early withdrawal penalty

Be aware that you generally can't claim more than one of these benefits for the same qualifying educational expense. It's best to compare all the potential benefits so you or your tax professional can choose the combination of tax credit(s) and deduction(s) that would result in the lowest tax bill possible. See IRS Publication 970, Tax Benefits for Education, for complete details at irs.gov.

10

Understanding Taxes

Intaxication: Euphoria at getting a refund from the IRS,
which lasts until you realize it was your money to start with.

—From a *Washington Post* word contest

Though many people (including me) gripe about paying taxes,
they're meant to make our lives better and safer by funding the
military, police, fire departments, public schools, and lots more. Since
so much of our income and accumulated wealth goes to the government, it's important to understand what we're shelling out in income taxes. But that's not an easy task. In case you're interested, at
the U.S. Government Printing Office at gpo.gov, you can download
all twenty volumes of the tax law—which is nearly 15,000 pages! I
doubt you want to read all that, so I'll tell you what you really need
to know in this chapter. There are easy strategies you can use to reduce your income and investment taxes. You'll learn how to legally
cut your tax bill and save money by taking advantage of tax deductions, tax credits, and tax-favored accounts.

TAXABLE VERSUS NONTAXABLE INCOME

Before we get into specifics on how income is taxed, let's determine
what type of income is subject to tax in the first place. Here are
some of the most common types of taxable income:

- Salaries and wages
- Tips
- Commissions and bonuses
- Interest
- Dividends
- Certain noncash fringe benefits
- Sick pay
- Severance pay
- Pensions and annuities
- Gambling winnings
- Prizes and awards
- Jury duty payments
- Unemployment compensation
- Certain federal payments such as Social Security, in some cases
- Royalties and licensing fees
- Bartering
- Canceled debts (not due to bankruptcy)
- Rent on property you lease
- Alimony received
- Traditional IRA withdrawals

Your gross income from all sources during the tax year is reduced by qualified adjustments, such as alimony payments and contributions to an IRA, and the final number is your adjusted gross income (AGI). Your modified adjusted gross income (MAGI) is your AGI with certain items added back in, such as foreign income or deductions for IRA contributions. MAGI is used to determine qualification for certain tax benefits as well as the Roth IRA income limits, for example.

The IRS doesn't get to take a cut of all your money, thank goodness. Here are some types of nontaxable income:

- Life insurance proceeds
- Health and accident benefits
- Disability income if policy premiums were taxed
- Child support received
- Gifts and inheritances you receive

- Cash rebates
- Rewards from credit card companies
- Worker's compensation
- Court damages received
- Federal income tax refunds
- Most education scholarships and fellowships
- Roth IRA qualified distributions
- Veterans Administration disability benefits
- Welfare and disaster relief grants
- Supplemental Security Income (SSI)
- Foster care for younger children
- Gain on the sale of personal residence (with restrictions up to a certain amount)
- Interest on certain state or municipal bonds

These aren't complete lists of taxable and nontaxable income, but I've included them so you know there are situations when you don't owe tax. However, be aware that the tax law treats various situations differently. For instance, if you surrender a life insurance policy for cash it may be taxable, but if you receive life insurance proceeds as a beneficiary it usually isn't taxable. When in doubt, it's best to seek the advice of an accountant or refer to IRS Publication 525, Taxable and Nontaxable Income.

CHOOSING THE BEST FILING STATUS

Any discussion of taxes should start with filing status. Each taxpayer must declare a filing status for your annual tax return and Form W-2 if you're an employee. Your filing status is based on your marital status and family situation. It determines important things like the amount of withholding from your paycheck and tax deductions and credits that you can take. (We'll cover all of that in this chapter.) Therefore, your filing status plays a big part in the amount of tax you'll owe.

There are five income tax filing statuses: Married Filing Jointly, Married Filing Separately, Single, Head of Household, and Qualifying Widow(er) with Dependent Child. You must choose one status for each tax year, so always choose the one that results in the least amount of tax. Here's a brief description of each one:

- **Married Filing Jointly status** applies if on the last day of the year you were legally married. Filing a joint return allows spouses to combine income, exemptions, and allowable deductions on one tax return. It gives you more tax benefits and usually results in lower taxes than filing separately.

- **Married Filing Separately status** applies if on the last day of the year you were legally married. It generally offers the least beneficial tax treatment, but may be necessary if one spouse doesn't agree with the other about taxes. For instance, one wants to file taxes but the other wants to skirt the law, or one spouse doesn't want to take joint responsibility for the other's tax messes. Even if you file separately, you still have to coordinate with your spouse on a couple of issues. If you have dependents, such as children or other adults that you care for, you'll have to decide who gets to claim them. Each dependent you claim lowers your taxable income (more about that coming up). And if one spouse itemizes deductions, the other must also itemize.

- **Single status** applies if on the last day of the year you were unmarried or were legally separated or divorced from your spouse. If you'll claim a dependent, check to see if Head of Household status may save you more in taxes.

- **Head of Household status** applies if you're considered unmarried on the last day of the year, paid more than half the cost of keeping up your home, and had a qualifying dependent live with you for more than half the year. This status gives you more tax benefit than filing as a single taxpayer or as a married person filing separately. But not every single parent qualifies for this status.

- **Qualifying Widow or Widower with Dependent Child status** applies if you're unmarried due to the death of your spouse within the last two years, and you've cared for a dependent all year. After two years, if you remain unmarried, your filing status must change to either Single or Head of Household.

For more information see IRS Publication 501, Exemptions, Standard Deduction, and Filing Information, at irs.gov.

WHO MUST FILE A TAX RETURN?

If you're wondering who has to file a federal tax return, the answer depends on the taxpayer's income, filing status, and age. (State filing requirements are different, so be sure check those at taxfoundation.org). If you're younger than sixty-five, you have to file a federal tax return if your gross income reaches these limits:

- Married Filing Jointly (if both spouses are younger than sixty-five): $18,700
- Married Filing Separately: $3,650
- Single: $9,350
- Head of Household: $12,000
- Qualifying Widow(er): $15,050

If you're older than sixty-five, you have to file a federal tax return if your gross income reaches these slightly higher limits:

- Married Filing Jointly (if one spouse is sixty-five or older): $19,800
- Married Filing Jointly (if both spouses are sixty-five or older): $20,900
- Married Filing Separately: $3,650
- Single: $10,750
- Head of Household: $13,400
- Qualifying Widow(er): $16,150

Even if you don't reach the above income limits, you may still need to file a return in order to get a tax refund that you're owed. Also, future years may be adjusted for inflation, so visit irs.gov for current information.

PAYROLL TAX WITHHOLDING

If you're like most people, you probably feel the bite from taxes when you see how much gets deducted from your gross paycheck. As I'm sure you know, when you land a job making $40,000, you don't actually get $40,000. The taxes that are automatically deducted are called withholding, because it's withheld from you and goes to the government instead. Withholding is a "pay-as-you-go" tax collection method that benefits the government because it reduces the likelihood of tax evasion. It puts the administrative burden of tax collection on employers who are required to calculate and submit income taxes on behalf of their employees. Employers are required to withhold four different kinds of taxes from employees' paychecks:

1. Federal income taxes
2. State income taxes
3. Social Security taxes
4. Medicare taxes

When you take a new job, one of the forms you complete is the W-4. That form tells your employer how much federal income tax should be taken out of your pay based on the number of allowances you claim. An allowance is the same as an exemption from tax. The more allowances you claim, the less federal income tax will be taken out of your paycheck. Adjustments to your income, such as claiming a child care tax credit, taking a student loan interest deduction, or receiving alimony, can affect your tax liability and should prompt you to review your withholding. You can file a new W-4 with your employer any time your personal situation changes, like if you get married, divorced, or have additional dependents.

Here's a quick and dirty tip: Use the Withholding Calculator at irs.gov or the W-4 Assistant at paycheckcity.com to help you fill out the W-4 form and to know when you should submit a revised one.

You adjust the number of allowances to avoid having too much or too little tax withheld. Your goal should be to have your withholding match the actual amount of tax you'll owe. If too little tax is withheld, you'll owe tax at the end of the year and may also have to pay interest plus a penalty for not paying on time. If too much tax is withheld, you lose the use of that money (when it could have been earning you interest) until the government gives you a refund.

> Here's a quick and dirty tip: Remember to review your tax withholding at the beginning of each year. Some employers send out a reminder notice about this, but others may not.

You also pay state income tax, unless you live in one of the nine states that don't collect it: Alaska, Florida, Nevada, New Hampshire, South Dakota, Tennessee, Texas, Washington, or Wyoming. (Two of those states, New Hampshire and Tennessee, only impose taxes on dividend and interest income.) Each state's tax rate is different—Oregon, New Jersey, and California impose some of the highest state rates. So visit taxfoundation.org for more information about your state's income tax rate.

The last two payroll taxes, Social Security and Medicare, are collectively called FICA. That stands for the Federal Insurance Contributions Act tax. The benefits provided by Social Security are summarized by the program's official name, OASDI, which stands for old-age, survivors, and disability insurance. Medicare is the federal program that provides hospital insurance benefits once you reach age sixty-five.

Many people don't realize that employers are also required to pay a matching amount of FICA for each of their employees with every paycheck. So the amount of Social Security retirement benefits that you receive is directly related to the amount that you and your various employers have paid into the program over your entire working career. In 2010, the tax rate for Social Security is 6.2 percent. So employers withhold that amount from your gross wages

Here's a quick and dirty tip: If you have more than one job and earn over the wage threshold for Social Security, you may have too much tax withheld. There's a line on Form 1040 for you to recover the excess.

in addition to paying another 6.2 percent of the company's money on your behalf. That tax is paid each year until a wage base threshold is reached—$106,800 for 2010. Once you earn that much, neither you nor your employer has to pay additional Social Security tax. The Medicare tax rate for 2010 is 1.45 percent. There is no wage base for the Medicare portion of FICA tax, so both the employee and the employer pay a combined total of 2.9 percent no matter how much is earned. Starting in 2013 Medicare taxes will increase for high-income households due to heath care legislation. Those who will be affected are individuals who earn more than $200,000 and couples who earn more than $250,000.

What's Estimated Tax?

If you don't pay tax through withholding, or don't pay enough, you're required to pay estimated tax. If you're self-employed, you generally have to make estimated tax payments four times a year. You might also need to make estimated tax payments if you have significant additional income from dividends, interest, capital gains, rent, royalties, alimony, and prizes, for instance.

THE SELF-EMPLOYMENT (SE) TAX

If you're self-employed, in addition to paying your federal and state taxes, you also pay the self-employment tax. The SE tax is both the employee and employer side of FICA tax for a grand total of 15.3 percent. That's 12.4 percent (6.2% + 6.2%) for the Social Security portion up to the wage threshold of $106,800 and 2.9 percent (1.45% + 1.45%) for the Medicare portion. The self-employment tax

Here's a quick and dirty tip: When you fail to report income you can be charged penalties, extra interest charges, or even be put in jail! Unreported income also doesn't get credited to your Social Security account, which reduces your income benefits during retirement.

can come as a big shock when you make the move from being an employee to working for yourself. As I mentioned, you generally must pay estimated taxes each quarter based on how much you think you'll earn, even if you're just working part-time at your business. That helps you stay on track with tax payments, so you don't spend money that really belongs to the government. Otherwise you could find yourself unprepared to pay a huge tax bill at the end of the year. I can tell you from personal experience that when you go into business, one of your new best friends should be a certified public accountant (CPA). He or she can help you calculate the amount you should pay in estimated quarterly taxes.

Even though you have to pay more in taxes when you're self-employed, you'll have the benefit of being able to deduct qualified business expenses. Those are all the common and necessary costs of running your business, such as office supplies, computer software, liability insurance, entertaining, or travel, for instance. You can deduct all or a portion of them from your taxable business income, which reduces the amount of tax you owe. You file self-employment tax on Schedule SE with Form 1040.

TAX BRACKETS

Tax rates for your ordinary income are a little tricky. That's because you're taxed by "tax brackets." A tax bracket is a range of income that's taxed at a unique rate. You pay a lower tax rate on your first dollars of income earned and a higher rate on your last dollars of income earned. You'd think that if you make $100,000 and you were in the 25 percent tax bracket, that you'd pay exactly $25,000 in taxes. I'm guilty of making flat calculations like that at times, to try to simplify examples that involve income tax. But your income is actually taxed at a progressive or marginal rate, which means that as your income increases, it's subject to increasing rates of each tax bracket. Your total marginal tax rate is the total of your federal and state rates, plus any local rates that may apply.

Take a look at the chart below and I'll give you an example to show you how federal taxes work.

FEDERAL INDIVIDUAL INCOME TAX RATES FOR 2010				
MARGINAL TAX RATE	MARRIED FILING JOINTLY	MARRIED FILING SEPARATELY	SINGLE	HEAD OF HOUSEHOLD
10%	Up to $16,750	Up to $8,375	Up to $8,375	Up to $11,950
15%	$16,751 to $68,000	$8,376 to $34,000	$8,376 to $34,000	$11,951 to $45,550
25%	$68,001 to $137,300	$34,001 to $68,650	$34,001 to $82,400	$45,551 to $117,650
28%	$137,301 to $209,250	$68,651 to $104,625	$82,401 to $171,850	$117,651 to $190,550
33%	$209,251 to $373,650	$104,626 to $186,825	$171,851 to $373,650	$190,551 to $373,650
35%	$373,651 or more	$186,826 or more	$373,651 or more	$373,651 or more

Let's say Caroline makes $100,000 in 2010, and she files income tax as a single person. Here's how her income tax bill is calculated:

Income Bracket	Amount	Tax Rate		Tax Due
$0–$8,375	$8,375	@ 10%	=	$837.50
$8,376–$34,000	$25,625	@ 15%	=	$3,843.75
$34,001–$82,400	$48,400	@ 25%	=	$12,100.00
$82,401–$100,000	$17,600	@ 28%	=	$4,928.00
TOTALS	$100,000			$21,709.00

Caroline's effective or average tax rate is actually 21.7 percent ($21,709 ÷ $100,000). She's only charged a marginal tax rate of 28 percent on the very highest amount of her income that falls into the 28 percent tax bracket, which is $17,600 ($100,000 – $82,401). In her situation, almost half of her income, $48,400, falls in the 25 percent bracket, so that's why her average tax rate turns out to be lower than her stated tax rate of 28 percent.

Check taxfoundation.org for up-to-date federal and state tax rates. They have a complete history of U.S. federal income tax rates that dates back to 1913.

HOW YOUR INVESTMENTS ARE TAXED

It's not just earnings from your job that get taxed; any money you make from your investments gets taxed, too. We've discussed how investments like bonds, bank savings accounts, and CDs pay you interest. That interest is taxed at your ordinary, marginal tax rate (see the 2010 tax rate chart above), even if you reinvest the money. So if you make a total of $500 in interest from your money market deposit account during the year, whether you withdraw that amount of money or leave it in the account to compound, you have to pay tax on it. Don't worry about keeping up with how much you've earned—you should receive a Form 1099-INT from each company that pays you interest after the end of the year.

Another type of investment income comes from stocks or funds that pay out a dividend. A dividend is a share of a company's profits that are divided among its shareholders. Some dividends are taxed as ordinary income (just like interest income), but most are taxed as a capital gain.

What Are Capital Gains?

Capital gains and losses are important tax concepts to grasp. You have a capital gain when you sell a capital asset—such as a stock or ETF—for a price that's higher that what it cost you. Conversely, you have a capital loss when you sell for a price lower than what you

Here's a quick and dirty tip: You don't pay capital gains tax on the first $250,000 of gain (or $500,000 if you file a joint return) on the sale of your personal residence if you lived there for at least two of the five years before the sale.

originally paid, so a capital gain or loss never exists until you sell a capital asset. For example, you can own shares of stock that grow in value over decades, but you don't pay tax on that growth until you decide to sell some or all of them. When you do sell a capital asset for a gain, you can offset it by capital losses, to reduce your tax liability (except in the case of losses on the sale of your personal residence). But you can only use up to $3,000 of losses to reduce your taxes each year. However, additional capital losses can be carried forward into future tax years.

A capital gain is taxed differently depending on how long you owned the capital asset that was sold. A short-term gain occurs if you own a capital asset for a year or less and a long-term gain occurs if you own it for more than a year. (Exceptions can include capital gain distributions paid by regulated investment companies, such as mutual funds and real estate investment trusts, which are generally always reported as long-term capital gains.) Long-term gains get favorable tax treatment; they're usually taxed at a lower rate than ordinary income and short-term gains. So if you take any information away from this section, it should be that long-term capital gains are preferable to ordinary income because they cost you less in taxes. After the end of the year, you should receive Form 1099-DIV for your dividend and capital gain distributions.

Here's a quick and dirty tip: Losses on investments that you haven't sold yet are called unrealized or paper losses. Until you sell a capital asset for a loss, you really haven't lost money!

Here are the capital gains tax rates:

FEDERAL INDIVIDUAL CAPITAL GAINS TAX RATES FOR 2010		
MARGINAL TAX RATE	SHORT-TERM GAIN	LONG-TERM GAIN
10%	10%	0%
15%	15%	0%
25%	25%	15%
28%	28%	15%
33%	33%	15%
35%	35%	15%

Keep in mind though that capital gains aren't as simple as the rates in the above chart, because there are exceptions (like for the sale of collectibles and real estate). Since the marginal and capital gains tax rates are sure to change in future years, refer to taxfoundation.org for the most current information.

TAKING TAX DEDUCTIONS

Want to know one of the best ways to legally reduce your tax bill? Take every single tax deduction that you can! A tax deduction is an amount that the IRS allows you to subtract from your taxable income, such as charitable contributions, student loan interest, and certain IRA contributions. When you reduce your taxable income, you also lower your tax liability. For example, if your taxable income is $40,000—but you're eligible to claim $10,000 in allowable deductions—then you only have to pay taxes on $30,000. That makes a huge difference. The IRS offers you two ways to calculate

 Here's a quick and dirty tip: Even though the maximum long-term capital gains tax rate is 15 percent, a winning stock investment in a Roth IRA could create significant tax savings due to the Roth's tax-free growth.

your deductions: taking a standard deduction or itemizing them. You choose the option that gives you the lowest tax bill and saves you the most money.

The Standard Deduction

Taking the standard deduction is easy because you don't have to gather any records or do any calculations—maybe that's why most taxpayers do it. But that doesn't mean it's going to save you the most tax money! The standard deduction is a fixed amount for each filing status that can change from year to year. Here are the amounts for 2010 (higher amounts apply to blind people and those over the age of sixty-five):

Married Filing Jointly	$11,400
Married Filing Separately	$5,700
Single	$5,700
Head of Household	$8,400
Qualifying Widow(er)	$11,400

Itemizing means that you add up all your actual deductions and claim them on Schedule A of Form 1040. If you file as Head of Household, for example, and have more than $8,400 in total deductions to itemize, you'll come out ahead as compared to taking the standard deduction. Be aware that some tax deductions are limited based on the amount of your adjusted gross income. Plus, there are some tax deductions that you can take even if you claim the standard deduction, such as the tuition and fees deduction. Always figure your taxes both ways and then choose the method that's most beneficial to you. Here are some allowable deductions that you may be able to take:

- Certain medical and dental expenses and insurance premiums
- State and local income taxes or general sales taxes
- Real estate taxes
- Interest paid on home mortgages
- Points paid on a home mortgage

Here's a quick and dirty tip: When you won't have enough deductions to exceed the standard deduction for the tax year, consider ways to delay payment for deductible expenses so you can take them in the next year instead.

- Mortgage insurance premiums
- Gifts to certain charitable organizations
- Casualty and theft losses
- Job expenses such as travel, dues, education
- Tax preparation fees
- Investment interest paid
- Gambling losses

You can't claim any of the above expenses if you were reimbursed for them or if they were paid by someone else. See Instructions for Schedule A for more details on allowable deductions.

Tax Exemptions

An exemption is a type of tax deduction that the IRS allows. As with other deductions, exemptions are wonderful because they reduce your taxable income, which reduces the total amount on which your tax rate is calculated. For 2010, you can deduct $3,650 for each exemption and there are two kinds: personal and dependents.

Personal exemptions include you and your spouse (if you have one and no one else can claim him or her as a dependent). Your spouse is never considered your dependent—at least for tax purposes, anyway! If you file a joint return, you can claim one exemption for yourself and one for your spouse—a total of $7,300 ($3,650 + $3,650). But if you're married and file separately, you can only claim an exemption for your spouse if they had no gross income and no one else can claim them as a dependent. If someone else, such as your parent, claims you as their dependent, you can't claim a personal exemption for yourself on your tax return.

Here's a quick and dirty tip: Always save receipts for your tax-deductible expenses or charitable donations. If you drop off clothes or household items to a charity collection center, ask for a receipt for the estimated value of your donation. Your charitable contributions are tax deductible when you itemize your deductions.

Each person can only be counted as an exemption once per tax year.

The dependent exemption is a tax break for each child or other allowable dependent that you may have (as long as no one else can claim them). If you're divorced or separated from a spouse, the parent who has custody of the child for more than half of the tax year can claim the child as a dependent; it doesn't matter which parent provided more financial support for the child during the year. See IRS Publication 501, Exemptions, Standard Deduction, and Filing Information, at irs.gov for tests to determine who can be claimed as a dependent.

TAKING TAX CREDITS

If you're starting to catch on to the benefits of tax deductions, there's something even better out there—tax credits. You've learned that tax deductions reduce the income on which your tax is calculated. Tax credits are even more exciting (if you like saving money as much as I do!) because they lower your actual tax. Tax credits are like gift cards from your Uncle Sam. Just like the way you use a retail store gift card to lower your total purchase at the checkout register, tax credits cut the amount of tax you owe. That makes them more valuable than deductions in most cases.

There are three different types of tax credits: refundable, nonrefundable, and partially refundable. For a refundable tax credit you're paid any excess as a tax refund. For example, if you don't owe any tax, but qualify for a refundable tax credit of $500, you'll receive a tax refund of $500. Or if you're already due a tax refund of $250, that same refundable $500 tax credit would increase your refund to $750.

Nonrefundable credits, on the other hand, only reduce your tax liability to zero. That's great when you owe tax, but a nonrefundable tax credit doesn't benefit you if you don't owe any tax or receive a tax refund.

The third type of tax credit is a partially refundable credit. A $1,000 tax credit that's 40 percent refundable means your refund could be a maximum amount of $400. So, for example, if you have a tax bill of $1,000, you'd owe zero, but if you owe zero, you'd only receive a $400 ($1,000×40%) refund.

Available tax credits change from year to year—that may be why many people miss out on taking advantage of them, even though they might qualify for several. Tax credits may involve filling out an extra tax form, but spending a little extra time researching available tax breaks can save you a lot of money. Stay alert to credits that may apply to your situation and check the home page at irs.gov for updates. See if you're eligible for some of these tax credits:

- **Child Tax Credit.** If you have a dependent child under the age of seventeen, you probably qualify for this credit. It can be as much as $1,000 per eligible child, and is in addition to the dependent exemption of $3,650 that was discussed in the prior section on tax deductions. You claim it on Form 1040 or on Form 8812, Additional Child Tax Credit. See IRS Publication 972 for complete information.

- **Child and Dependent Care Credit.** If you have a child under the age of thirteen or other adult dependents and pay someone to care for them so you can work (or look for work), you probably qualify for this credit. You claim it on Form 2441, Child and Dependent Care Expenses, or on Form 1040A. See IRS Publication 503 for complete information.

- **Adoption Credit.** If you adopt a child under the age of eighteen, you may qualify for this credit. Use Form 8839, Qualified Adoption Expenses, and send it in with Form 1040.

- **Earned Income Tax Credit (EITC).** The EITC helps low and moderate-income taxpayers. The amount of income earned and family size determine the amount of the credit (although you don't have to have children to qualify). The IRS says that one in six taxpayers is eligible for this credit. Use the EITC Assistant at irs.gov and see IRS Publication 596 for complete information.

- **Credit for the Elderly and Disabled.** This credit helps those who are disabled or those over the age of sixty-five. There are strict income limits that apply. You claim this credit on Form 1040. See IRS Publication 524 for complete information.

- **Retirement Savings Contribution Credit.** This credit helps low and moderate-income taxpayers who make contributions to an IRA or certain workplace retirement plans. See IRS Publication 590 for complete information.

- **American Opportunity Tax Credit.** This credit is available for qualified expenses for higher education—such as books, supplies, coursework materials, and a computer that's necessary for school enrollment—for the 2009 and 2010 tax years. The credit pays up to $2,500 and is 40 percent refundable. You claim it by submitting IRS Form 8863 with your tax return. Check irs.gov to find out if this credit gets extended for tax years after 2010. See chapter 9 for more about this credit and IRS Publication 970 for complete information.

- **Lifetime Learning Credit.** This credit is up to $2,000 for education even when the student isn't pursuing a degree. He or she can take just one course at an eligible institution to qualify for an unlimited number of tax years. See chapter 9 for more about this credit and IRS Publication 970 for complete information.

- **Nonbusiness Energy Property Credit.** This is available for a percentage of the cost of certain improvements to an existing home placed into service by the end of 2010, such as energy-efficient

Here's a quick and dirty tip: In addition to federal tax credits for energy efficiency, you may also qualify for state tax breaks or rebates from your utility company. There's a full list of all energy incentives at the Database of State Incentives for Renewables & Efficiency at dsire.us.org.

roofs; air conditioners; heat pumps; water heaters; exterior windows, skylights, doors; and insulation. You claim it on Form 5695, Residential Energy Credits, and send it in with your return.

- **Residential Energy Efficient Property Credit.** This credit encourages investment in alternative energy equipment, placed into service by the end of 2016, such as solar electric systems, solar water heaters, geothermal heat pumps, fuel cell property, and wind turbines. It's available for a percentage of the cost of these improvements to existing and new homes. You claim it on Form 5695, Residential Energy Credits, and send it in with your return.

THE ALTERNATIVE MINIMUM TAX

Many people aren't aware of the Alternative Minimum Tax (AMT), which was introduced in 1969 to ensure that all taxpayers pay at least a minimum amount of federal tax. Unfortunately, the AMT kicks in when you have a high amount of itemized tax deductions or tax credits that significantly lower your taxes. The AMT system is like a parallel tax universe with its own tax rates, broader definition of taxable income, and reduced number of exemptions and deductions. It identifies taxpayers who take advantage of legal tax breaks and forces them to completely recalculate their tax. That's done by (1) adding back in certain income that's considered nontaxable under the regular system, (2) taking a special AMT exemption, and (3) recalculating tax based on different, flat rates.

You have to figure what you owe for both the regular system and the AMT system and then pay the higher amount. Yes, the AMT is very confusing—so I recommend that you use the AMT As-

Here's a quick and dirty tip: IRS Publication 17, Your Federal Income Tax for Individuals, covers the general rules for filing a federal income tax return. You can refer to it at irs.gov to make sure that you don't pay more than is necessary.

sistant at irs.gov. It's a test to determine if you need to pay the AMT. If you use software to complete your return, it should automatically determine whether or not you're subject to the AMT. You can figure it manually on IRS Form 6251 if needed.

HOW TO CHOOSE A TAX PRO

If you weren't already convinced that tax preparation is confusing, I'm sure the previous section on the AMT changed your mind! If your tax situation is even the least bit complicated, I strongly recommend that you use a qualified tax professional. They do cost money (though probably not as much as you think), but they can also help you save money. There's no government regulation for tax preparers—anyone can print a business card, put out a shingle, and call themselves a tax preparer! Therefore, it's important to be familiar with the different professionals who are available to help you. Each type of tax preparer has varying levels of experience and suitability for your situation. Here are the main types of tax professionals:

- Tax preparer from national chains or local outlets
- Enrolled agent
- Certified public accountants
- Tax attorney

The professionals at the national tax preparation chains or similar businesses are trained to some extent, but their training and experience could vary. They may not be paid much more than minimum wage plus commission, and may be preparing tax returns as a second job. If your return is a fairly simple one, then a franchise service could be an appropriately inexpensive option. They can accompany you to a meeting with the Internal Revenue Service to help you explain information on your return, if needed. However, only enrolled agents, attorneys, and CPAs have legal standing to appear in place of a taxpayer at the IRS. If your return is at all complex, or you have tax situations specific to your industry, some of the franchise preparers may not maximize your deductions.

An enrolled agent (EA) is licensed by the federal government, and is either a former IRS employee or someone who's passed a comprehensive IRS exam. If there are questions about your return, an enrolled agent can represent you with the IRS. Many enrolled agents limit their work to a given tax area, so be sure to inquire about their area of expertise. You can get assistance and referrals from the National Association of Enrolled Agents at naea.org.

A certified public accountant (CPA) has passed a state's qualifying exam for accounting, but may or may not be an expert on tax matters. The strength of a CPA is that they can configure an overall tax plan and guide you through complex financial situations. If you're recently married, divorced, retired, opened or closed a new business, or had any other lifestyle changes that significantly impact your financial situation, a CPA may be your best option. Be sure, however, to ask about his or her tax experience and how they keep up with changes in the tax law. Also, a CPA can represent you before the IRS. The American Institute of Certified Public Accountants' Web page at aicpa.org has more information.

A tax attorney may be your best choice if your situation involves complex personal or corporate matters. A tax attorney may specialize on the latest tax law, but be less qualified in the preparation of actual returns, so inquire about his or her experience. Visit the American Bar Association at abanet.org to find tax attorneys in your area.

Here are eight tips from the IRS to help you choose a tax professional that's best for you:

1. **Check the person's qualifications.** Ask if the preparer is affiliated with a professional organization that provides its

members with continuing education and resources and holds them to a code of ethics.

2. **Check on the preparer's history.** Check to see if the preparer has any questionable history with the Better Business Bureau, the state's board of accountancy for CPAs, or the state's bar association for attorneys.

3. **Find out about their service fees.** Avoid preparers that base their fee on a percentage of the amount of your refund or those who claim they can obtain larger refunds than other preparers.

4. **Make sure the tax preparer is accessible.** Make sure you'll be able to contact the tax preparer after the return has been filed, even after April 15, in case questions arise.

5. **Provide all records and receipts needed to prepare your return.** Most reputable preparers will request to see your records and receipts and will ask you multiple questions to determine your total income and your qualifications for expenses, deductions, and other items.

6. **Never sign a blank return.** Avoid tax preparers that ask you to sign a blank tax form.

7. **Review the entire return before signing it.** Before you sign your tax return, review it and ask questions. Make sure you understand everything and are comfortable with the accuracy of the return before you sign it.

8. **Make sure the preparer signs the form.** A paid preparer must sign the return as required by law. The preparer must also give you a copy of the return. Although the preparer signs the return, you are responsible for the accuracy of every item on your return.

Conclusion:
20 Tips for Putting It All Together

If you've read this far, we've covered a lot of territory together. If there were any topics that you struggled with, I hope you'll go back and reread them because I want you to get the most you can out of this book. Putting new plans in place will probably mean doing things that feel a little uncomfortable for a while. But stretching yourself to new limits is a part of how you grow and create a better life for yourself and those you love.

Here are some final tips to help you put it all together and make the smart moves necessary to grow rich.

Tip #1: Analyze Your Money Mind-set

Be honest with yourself about your relationship with money. In many cases your financial habits are deeply rooted in your emotional and psychological makeup. If you have friends or family members who've been successful with their personal finances, ask them for guidance. They may help you see your situation from a fresh perspective. Or seek the advice of a financial adviser, a professional counselor, or a coach to take control of your situation.

Tip #2: Save First, Spend Later

Success starts by making saving a priority over spending. It's smart to fund your savings and investments first, before spending money on anything else. The amount you save should be determined within the context of your income and overall financial goals.

Tip #3: Keep Score for Best Results

Measuring your financial progress is an integral part of making improvements. Establish a financial baseline by creating your Personal Financial Statement, and update it on a quarterly basis. Your financial decisions up to this point got you where you are today. Don't dwell on the past. Simply decide that in order for change to occur, change must occur! Keep track of your financial score by monitoring your net worth.

Tip #4: Make More and Spend Less

Most people instinctively spend more when they make more. When you can widen the gap between your income and your living expenses, you're left with more discretionary income—an incredibly powerful tool. Fortunes can be grown from the seed of discretionary income. It's the secret to building wealth and having enough to provide for all your financial goals.

Tip #5: Build Your Banking Dream Team

Your bank and credit accounts are your financial team; they should work hard for you. Get rid of the duds and replace them with better-performing options. Always be ready to upgrade and restructure your banking or credit cards when there's a more efficient or profitable way to manage your money. Whether it's an online savings account or a rewards credit card, rates and benefits can change. Make it a habit to shop around and to stay alert for better banking and credit alternatives.

Tip #6: Tackle Debts in the Best Possible Order

Get rid of your debts according to the risk they pose to you and your family. For credit cards and loans, always eliminate those with the highest interest rates first. Reduce your liabilities in this order:

1. Debts that can get you into legal trouble such as unpaid child support, legal judgments, or tax delinquencies
2. Debts that are in default and already in the hands of a collections agency
3. Credit cards or high-interest loans
4. Lower-interest loans with no tax deduction
5. Lower-interest loans that come with a tax deduction

Tip #7: Crack Down on Credit Card Debt

Getting rid of high-interest credit card debt is one of the best ways to improve your personal finances. The habit of only paying a card's monthly minimum balance costs you a lot in interest and only prolongs the agony of having to repay it. The longer you carry a credit card balance, the bigger the financial monster gets, and the more difficult it is to slay it.

Tip #8: Pay Credit Card Balances Biweekly

Each time you make a purchase with a credit card, log that expense in your check register as if you just paid for the item with a check or debit card. Then pay the accumulated balance to the credit card company in full every other week so you won't be tempted to overspend with plastic.

Tip #9: Pay Installment Loans Biweekly

If you get a regular paycheck, paying half of the monthly payment amount for your home, car, or student loan every other week is an easy way to save interest and pay off debt faster. Biweekly payments are a painless way to make a full extra payment each year.

Tip #10: Don't Underestimate the Need for an Emergency Fund

Financial advisers used to recommend that you save enough emergency money to cover two to three months' worth of expenses. The recent recession has been a harsh reminder that we need to keep more on hand to stay safe. Job losses, waning home equity, and shriveled-up credit lines make saving six months to a year's worth of living expenses in a low-risk account, a new common-sense financial requirement.

Tip #11: Slow and Steady Wins the Race

Investing the same amount on a consistent basis, or dollar-cost averaging, may seem boring, but it's actually a savvy strategy to reduce market risk. Buying small amounts over time of an investment, such as a mutual fund or ETF, is an affordable, convenient, and effective way to build long-term wealth.

Tip #12: Don't Fall for a Scam

It's not uncommon for intelligent people to fall prey to scams. Oftentimes scam victims have a feeling that something isn't right, but they go against their gut instinct. Only choose investments that you fully understand. Look out for the ways that con artists use to deceive people:

- They make you think their offer is unique to you
- They attempt to associate themselves with a trustworthy institution such as a church, a reputable business, or a well-known brand
- They ask you to comply with a small request that causes you to feel committed
- They offer something free (such as a lunch) that makes you feel obligated
- They promise investment returns that are unnaturally high or steady

- They utilize peer pressure by claiming that others in your group are already in
- They create a false sense of urgency by claiming an opportunity is available for a limited time or for a limited number of people only

Tip #13: Make Reallocation a Snap

Investment allocation is an important concept to grasp, but isn't as difficult to implement as it sounds. Take advantage of target-date, or life-cycle, mutual funds and ETFs to get the job done. They keep the right mix of asset classes for the average investor with a particular retirement date in mind. As the target date approaches, the fund shifts the underlying investments to more conservative options.

Tip #14: Never Pass Up Matching Funds

Employer-sponsored plans are one of the most advantageous ways to save for retirement. Automatic payroll deductions make it easy to invest and, over time, compound interest and tax-deferred growth can add up to a tidy sum. When combined with company matching, they can turbocharge your returns and investing power. If your company offers matching funds, always participate and contribute at least an amount that allows you to get the full amount of matching offered. Otherwise you're leaving money on the table.

Tip #15: IRA Is Your Friend

An IRA should be in everyone's investment portfolio because it's available to anyone who has taxable income. Even if you don't have taxable earnings, but are married and file a joint tax return, you can fund a spousal IRA.

Tip #16: Don't Take Early Withdrawals

Taking an early withdrawal from a retirement account should never be done except in extremely grim financial circumstances. If you're younger than fifty-nine and a half, it comes with an expensive penalty and leaves you poorly prepared for your future financial needs. In some situations, with professional guidance, it may be better to set up a 72(t) plan to establish substantially equal periodic payments.

Tip #17: Utilize Real Estate Professionals

Buying a home is a big decision and requires a lot of work to properly manage all the tasks that must be accomplished in a short period of time. Remember that everything is negotiable and a good real estate agent can save you time and money whether you're a buyer or a seller.

Tip #18: You Better Shop Around

Getting a mortgage is an expensive commitment that you should shop for carefully. Slight differences in interest rates make a big difference in the amount of interest you'll pay over the life of a long-term loan.

Tip #19: Don't Be a Dunce When Paying for Education

Federal student aid is the least expensive and most flexible way to pay for the cost of education. But you can't get approved for a federal loan, grant, fellowship, or work-study program without completing the FAFSA. Many people who are qualified to receive aid don't get it because they fail to submit the application.

Tip #20: Set It, But Don't Forget It

Automate as much of your money management as possible. For example, have your workplace split your paycheck deposit into a payment account and a savings account. Use online bill pay and auto-payments to save time and effort. Set up automatic transfers into an investment account, such as an IRA, to make sure the job of investing gets done first. Review and adjust your savings and investment plan at least once a year.

LET'S STAY IN TOUCH

I want to congratulate you for taking action to improve your personal finances and reading this book. I hope it's provided you with the information, tools, and resources you need to become a great money manager and a better architect of your financial future. I encourage you to continue to pursue your financial education every way that you can. Of course, the *Money Girl* podcast is a great way to do that because you'll always hear up-to-date and relevant financial information. If you're not familiar with podcasts yet, they're audio or video files you get over the Internet instead of from a radio or television. *Money Girl* is a weekly audio show that you can listen to for free at iTunes, the Zune Marketplace, or on the Quick and Dirty Tips Network (QDT) Web site at quickanddirtytips.com. You can download the iTunes player software for your PC or Mac for free at itunes.com. It includes a store where you can download music, videos, television shows, and free podcasts. On the *Money Girl* blog at http://moneygirl.quickanddirtytips.com, you'll find multiple ways to contact me. Remember that there are ways to get more money tips, financial resources, and information for free! Take a few moments *right now* to do the following:

FREE ACTION STEPS

- **Get thank-you gifts** for reading this book at smartmovestogrowrich .com! You can watch videos, sign up for my newsletter, and get more financial information.
- **Join the Money Girl Facebook page** at facebook.com/MoneyGirl QDT.
- **Follow me on Twitter** at twitter.com/lauraadams.
- **Subscribe to the Money Girl podcast** via RSS at http://moneygirl .quickanddirtytips.com or at iTunes.
- **Subscribe to Money Girl blog articles** via RSS at http://moneygirl .quickanddirtytips.com.

- **Share your financial questions and successes** with me by e-mail at money@quickanddirtytips.com.
- **Find information on topics that interest you** in the archives at quick anddirtytips.com.

I look forward to hearing from you!

Acknowledgments

I want to thank Mignon Fogarty, the founder of Quick and Dirty Tips (QDT), for taking a chance and inviting me to take over as the host of *Money Girl*. Your groundbreaking success with *Grammar Girl*, the QDT network, and your books has been a true inspiration to me. Without loyal *Money Girl* listeners and blog readers, this book wouldn't exist. So I also need to extend special gratitude to each and every fan who continues to download weekly podcasts from platforms like iTunes and to visit the *Money Girl* blog. Your encouraging e-mails, voice-mail messages, and Facebook comments are really what keep a podcaster going. Your questions and concerns motivate me to give you and the entire *Money Girl* community well-researched and timely financial advice.

There are many people on the Macmillan team who made this book a reality. Richard Rhorer, I can't thank you enough for your vote of confidence. Your progressive business vision, marketing expertise, and willingness to experiment with digital media have enlightened me. I am very fortunate to have the editing brilliance of Emily Rothschild behind this book as well as the weekly *Money Girl* column. Your advice and comments are always spot-on and exactly what's needed to improve my work.

To my family: Thanks for giving me the love, support, and education that's helped me succeed in life. My parents, Bud and Bonnie Doty, always put my needs and wants ahead of their own. How can that ever be repaid? Lastly, I have to thank my husband and best friend, Adam, who's always shown an amazing belief in me, kept my spirits up, and been ready to celebrate anything at a moment's notice. Even when the alarm clock went off way too early in the morning so I could write this book, he kept his sense of humor intact and never really complained about it. Any success I have is truly a tribute to you. I only hope that I have returned and will continue to reciprocate the love and support that you've given me.

Index

About the Author

Laura D. Adams is the host of *Money Girl* on Macmillan's Quick and Dirty Tips™ digital media network. She shares weekly tips and advice on a variety of personal finance topics. Her experience as an entrepreneur, a real estate investor, a corporate sales and marketing trainer, a human resources professional, and an instructional designer enriches her writing and brings vast experience to her audience.

Laura was born in Charleston, South Carolina. She received a B.S. in Natural Resources from The University of the South in Sewanee, Tennessee, and an MBA from the University of Florida. She lives in central Florida with her husband and their yellow Lab. To contact Laura, please visit the *Money Girl* Web site at http://moneygirl.quickanddirtytips.com or smartmovestogrowrich.com.

Quick and Dirty Tips™

Helping you do things better.

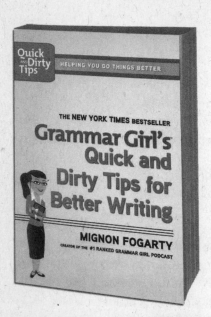

St. Martin's Griffin